GW00319430

Daily Readings From:
HIND'S FEET
ON HIGH PLACES

Given to: _____

On: _____

By: _____

With this special message:

_____

_____

_____

_____

One-Minute Devotions

Hind's Feet on High places

HANNAH HURNARD

CHRISTIAN ART
Vereeniging

HIND'S FEET ON HIGH PLACES

ISBN 1-86852-055-2

Printed in Singapore.

JANUARY

JANUARY 1

HIGH PLACES

*The Lord God is my strength,
and he will make my feet like
hinds' feet, and he will make me
to walk upon mine high places.*
Habakkuk 3:19 KJV

Every acceptance of his will becomes
an altar of sacrifice, and every such sur-
render and abandonment of ourselves to
his will is a means of furthering us on
the way to the High Places to which he
desires to bring every child of his while
they are still living on earth.

JANUARY 2

GOD IS WITH YOU

Yes, be bold and strong! Banish fear and doubt! For remember, the Lord your God is with you wherever you go.
Joshua 1:9 TLB

Never for a moment shall I be beyond your reach or call for help, even when you cannot see me ... I shall be present with you all the time, even though invisible.

JANUARY 3

HEAVENLY PLACES

*They that wait upon the Lord shall
renew their strength. They shall
mount up with wings like eagles;
they shall run and not by weary;
they shall walk and not faint.*
Isaiah 40:31 TLB

We are meant to enjoy the winged life
of those who have access to the heavenly places just as truly as the birds have
access to the sky.

JANUARY 4

FOLLOW ME

*He saith unto them, Follow me,
and I will make you fishers of
men. And they straightway left
their nets, and followed him.*
Matthew 4:19-20 KJV

I heard the call, "Come Follow." That
was all. Earth's joys grew dim, My soul
went after him, I rose and followed –
That was all.

JANUARY 5

ETERNAL LIFE

I give them eternal life, and they shall never perish; no one can snatch them out of my hand. My Father, who has given them to me, is greater than all.
John 10:28-29 NIV

There is no question of your turning back, Much-Afraid. No one, not even your own shrinking heart, can pluck you out of my hand.
– The Shepherd

JANUARY 6

ROOTS IN HEAVEN

*God has chosen poor people
to be rich in faith, and the
Kingdom of heaven is theirs.*
James 2:5 TLB

The meek of the earth already live in heaven. That is to say they have their roots in heaven, though for a little while longer their bodies are in the material world and subject to pain and death.

JANUARY 7

DAILY TESTIMONY

Do not be ashamed to testify about our Lord ... but join with me in suffering for the gospel, by the power of God, who saved us and called us to a holy life.
2 Timothy 1:8-9 NIV

For the simple, daily work of talking to others about the Savior of the world, you and I by God's grace, may be just the people he needs and can use.

JANUARY 8

HE IS FAITHFUL

Let us hold unswervingly to the hope we profess, for he who promised is faithful.
Hebrews 10:23 NIV

She had an inner vision of the face of the Shepherd. She remembered the look with which he had promised her. "I pledge myself to bring you there, and that you will not be put to shame."

JANUARY 9

TO LOVE TRULY

*Set your hearts on things above,
where Christ is seated at the right
hand of God. Set your minds on
things above, not on earthly things.*
Colossians 3:1-2 NIV

Love is the law of the winged life. Up
there in the heavenly places is to be experienced the perfect freedom and joy
of those who have learned to love truly
and have received power to do so continually and under all circumstances.

JANUARY 10

TRIUMPH IN CHRIST

Now thanks be unto God, which always causeth us to triumph in Christ, and maketh manifest the savour of his knowledge by us in every place.
2 Corinthians 2:14 KJV

The peaks speak of the high places of faith to which he wants to lead us in order that we may pour ourselves down with life-bringing joy to others, so our daily walk is to be like flower-filled fields offering beauty, comfort, cheer and encouragement.

JANUARY 11

ACT IN LOVE

Let us stop saying we love people; let us really love them, and show it by our actions.
1 John 3:18 TLB

Real love is not primarily a feeling at all, but a thing of the will. A determination to act as I would if I felt all the delight of loving deeply and happily ... If one acts in love, sooner or later one comes to feel all the joy and ecstasy of love.

PRAYER

*Pray in the Spirit on all occasions
with all kinds of prayers and requests.
With this in mind, be alert and always
keep on praying for all the saints.*
Ephesians 6:18 NIV

One startling and challenging fact
emerges, that many of the Lord's people in every part of the world are drearily conscious of something vitally
wrong with their prayer life.

PRACTISE KINDNESS

*Practise tenderhearted mercy
and kindness to others.*
Colossians 3:12 TLB

The flowers speak of the beautiful loving-kindnesses and tender mercies which he wants to shower on others through us.

JANUARY 14

A NEW LIFE

*When someone becomes a
Christian he becomes a brand new
person inside. He is not the same
anymore. A new life has begun!*
2 Corinthians 5:17 TLB

When the whole realm of the mind and
thought life passes out of the control
of self altogether, and becomes the kingdom of our Lord and Savior, Holy Love
himself, how complete and radiant is the
transformation.

THE KINGDOM OF HEAVEN

Let love and faithfulness never leave you; bind them around your neck, write them on the tablet of your heart.
Proverbs 3:3 NIV

Remember, the Kingdom of Heaven is everywhere where the law of love is practised and perfectly obeyed and where I, who am the King of Love, reign.

JANUARY 16

PRIDE

*When pride comes, then
comes disgrace, but with
humility comes wisdom.*
Proverbs 11:2 NIV

Once Pride is listened to, struggle as
one may, it is the hardest thing in the
world to throw him off.

JANUARY 17

HE IS THE TRUE GOD

We know that the Son of God has come and has given us understanding so that we may know him who is true; and we are in him who is true, in his Son Jesus Christ. He is the true God and eternal life.
1 John 5:20 NRSV

They who love most, see most. Love opens the eyes of our understanding and enables us to see more of the truth than can those who are blinded by self-love.

JANUARY 18

A NEW DISCOVERY

*Dear friends, build yourselves
up in your most holy faith and
pray in the Holy Spirit.*
Jude 20 NIV

Our Lord is longing to help us to a
new discovery, or rather rediscovery of
an entirely different and gloriously powerful ministry, through prayer and intercession, and wonders why we are so slow
and unwilling to be shown it!

JANUARY 19

THE PATH

The steps of good men are directed by the Lord. He delights in each step they take. If they fall it isn't fatal, for the Lord holds them with his hand.
Psalm 37:23-24 TLB

He looked at her and answered very gently, "That is the path, Much-Afraid, and you are to go down there." ... He was leading her away from her heart's desire altogether and gave no promise at all as to when he would bring her back.

JANUARY 20

WITHOUT LOVE

*For God hath not given us the spirit
of fear; but of power, and of
love, and of a sound mind.*
2 Timothy 1:7 KJV

Without love we can no more transmit
God's life and thoughts and power and
love to others, than our radio sets can
transmit when the current is turned off.

JANUARY 21

BE STRONG

*Be strong in the Lord and
in his mighty power. Put
on the full armor of God.*
Ephesians 6:10-11 NIV

Natural strength is often as great a
handicap as natural weakness; both must
be utterly yielded to the Lord.

THE KING OF KINGS

God, the blessed and only Ruler,
the King of kings and Lord of lords,
who alone is immortal and who lives
in unapproachable light, whom no
one has seen or can see.
1 Timothy 6:15-16 NIV

Hark! Such songs of jubilation!
Every creature sings.
Great is the joy of every nation.
"Love is King of kings."

JANUARY 23

THE LOVE OF CHRIST

I pray that you, being rooted and established in love, may have power, together with all the saints, to grasp how wide and long and high and deep is the love of Christ.
Ephesians 3:17-18 NIV

He helps me to understand at last the reason why we are born into this fallen world ... It is that we may learn, in a way which perhaps we could not do in heaven, how to abandon ourselves to loving God.

YIELD EVERYTHING

I urge you, brothers, in view of God's mercy, to offer your bodies as living sacrifices, holy and pleasing to God – this is your spiritual act of worship.
Romans 12:1 NIV

My Lord said, "There is just one secret of success, Hannah; you must accept it with joy, and determine to go all lengths in yielding every right ... Yield everything."

JANUARY 25

LEARN OF ME

Take my yoke upon you, and learn of me; for I am meek and lowly in heart: and ye shall find rest unto your souls.
Matthew 11:29 KJV

I can make you what I planned that you should be when I created you. If you will be meek and lowly of heart and learn of me, I will teach you.

JANUARY 26

LOVING-KINDNESS

*Great is his faithfulness; his
loving-kindness begins afresh
each day. My soul claims the
Lord as my inheritance.*
Lamentations 3:23-24 TLB

But every worshiping, grateful soul
thrills with awe and delight and wonder
at the daily blessings and loving-
kindnesses of the Creator Father.

JANUARY 27

SORROW

Godly sorrow brings repentance that leads to salvation and leaves no regret.
2 Corinthians 7:10 NIV

Sorrow seems able to put into our hands a golden key which can unlock to us treasures of truth and new understanding, far more often and more fully than joy can do.

JANUARY 28

I PLEDGE MYSELF

*No one who believes in
Christ will ever be disappointed.*
Romans 10:11 TLB

My Peace I leave with you. My Joy be
fulfilled in you. Remember that I pledge
myself to bring you to the High Places
at the top of these mountains and that
you shall not be put to shame.

JANUARY 29

AN INTERCESSOR

Those who are wise will shine like the brightness of the heavens, and those who lead many to righteousness like the stars for ever and ever.
Daniel 12:3 NIV

An intercessor means one who is in such vital contact with God and with his fellow men that he is like a live wire closing the gap between the saving power of God and the sinful men who have been cut off from that power.

THE RIGHT TO CHOOSE

*The man of integrity walks securely ...
the righteous stand firm forever.*
Proverbs 10:9, 25 NIV

I will go down with you into the wilderness ... I will go with you, for you know I do love you, and you have the right to choose for me anything that you please. – Much-Afraid

JANUARY 31

REVIVAL

Revive us, and we will call on your name. Restore us, O Lord God Almighty; make your face shine upon us, that we may be saved.
Psalm 80:18-19 NIV

Perhaps the long-prayed-for revival throughout the whole Church waits for the time when God's people enter radiantly and thankfully, yes, and adventurously, into this glorious ministry of intercession.

FEBRUARY

FEBRUARY 1

THE POTTER

The potter formed it into another pot, shaping it as seemed best to him ... "Like clay in the hand of the potter, so are you in my hand."
Jeremiah 18:4, 6 NIV

Thou art the mighty Potter, And I the yielding clay. Bend me, Oh bend me to thy will, While in thine hand I'm lying still.

WALK HUMBLY

*He hath showed thee, O man,
what is good; and what doth the
Lord require of thee, but to do
justly, and to love mercy, and to
walk humbly with thy God.*
Micah 6:8 KJV

We are in a perfect environment for learning how to love as God loves: to abandon ourselves to loving the apparently unlovely people who remind us that in many ways we are still very unlovely ourselves!

FEBRUARY 3

THE KINGDOM

Giving thanks to the Father, who has enabled you to share in the inheritance of the saints in the light. He has rescued us from the power of darkness and transferred us into the kingdom of his beloved Son.
Colossians 1:12-13 NRSV

It is God's purpose to translate us into the kingdom of his dear Son, now here on earth, and that it is most gloriously possible to be, as it were, annexed to heaven, even before we leave the body.

FEBRUARY 4

AN HONEST ESTIMATE

Be honest in your estimate of your-selves, measuring your value by how much faith God has given you.
Romans 12:3 TLB

Humility is simply to see yourselves as you really are, and meekness is to admit the truth about yourselves and to act accordingly.

FEBRUARY 5

HIS PROMISES

*For no matter how many
promises God has made,
they are "Yes" in Christ.*
2 Corinthians 1:20 NIV

One may catch one's breath as one be
gins the challenging ascent in one of his
promises, looking forward to what
seems an awfully dangerous precipice ...
But the promises are sure.

FEBRUARY 6

THE OPPORTUNITY

Joseph said to them, "Don't be afraid ... You intended to harm me, but God intended it for good to accomplish what is now being done, the saving of many lives."
Genesis 50:19-20 NIV

The greater the evil, the greater the opportunity to fashion out of it everlasting good. There are no circumstances allowed to come into the lives of God's own children which cannot be transformed into ultimate blessing.

HE DELIVERED ME

Glorify the Lord with me; let us exalt his name together. I sought the Lord, and he answered me; he delivered me from all my fears.
Psalm 34:3-4

Will he who is so strong and gentle be less faithful and gracious to me, weak and cowardly though I am, when it is so obvious that the thing he delights in most of all is to deliver his followers from all their fears and to take them to the High Places?

FEBRUARY 8

FORGIVENESS

Bear with each other and forgive whatever grievances you may have against one another. Forgive as the Lord forgave you.
Colossians 3:13 NIV

We see a great deal more meaning in the word forgiveness when we ourselves pass through the experience of being deeply wronged and have been taught by the Great Forgiver how to forgive and bear the wrong done to us.

UP AGAIN

*I am God ... fear not to go down
into Egypt ... I will go down with
thee into Egypt; and I will also
surely bring thee up again.*
Genesis 46:3-4 KJV

Those who come down to the furnace
go on their way afterwards as royal men
and women, princes and princesses of the
Royal Line.

FEBRUARY 10

FOLLOW ME

*Whoever serves me must follow
me, and where I am, there will
my servant be also. Whoever
serves me, the Father will honor.*
John 12:26 NRSV

Entreat me not to leave thee, Lord,
For Oh, I love thee so,
And where thou goest, Lord of Love
There will I also go.

FEBRUARY 11

ENDLESS LOVE

*Praise your name for your love and
faithfulness ... The Lord will fulfill
his purpose for me; your love, O
Lord, endures forever – do not
abandon the works of your hands.*
Psalm 138:2, 8 NIV

His endless, patient love never gives up.
It will never fail. How skillful he is. No-
body teaches as he does.

FEBRUARY 12

IN THE REALM OF LOVE

*Come, let us go up to the mountain of
the Lord ... He will teach us his ways,
so that we may walk in his paths.*
Micah 4:2 NIV

How many of us yearn to live actually
in the realm of love, to be at home in
the heavenly places, instead of having to
strain painfully and wearily in order to
enjoy for a few moments an experience
which we know ought to be habitual to
the children of God!

FEBRUARY 13

THE SHADOW
OF YOUR WINGS

*Show me the wonder of your
great love, you who save by your
right hand those who take refuge in
you from their foes. Keep me as the
apple of your eye; hide me in
the shadow of your wings.*
Psalm 17:7-8 NIV

Love is not a feeling. It is an overwhelming passion to help and bless and
deliver and comfort and strengthen and
give joy to others just as the Lord Jesus
always did.

FEBRUARY 14

TO LOVE

*Serve one another in love. The
entire law is summed up in a
single command: "Love your
neighbor as yourself."*
Galatians 5:13-14 NIV

All the practical teaching our Lord
gave in connection with the lives we are
to live here on earth was summed up in
the commandment to love.

FEBRUARY 15

FAITH IS OBEDIENCE

*Those who have served well gain
an excellent standing and great assurance in their faith in Chirst Jesus.*
1 Timothy 3:13 NIV

Faith has nothing to do with intellectual belief. Faith is obedience. Faith and
abandonment to God's will and power
are inseparable.

FEBRUARY 16

MORE LOVE

And the ransomed of the Lord shall return, and come to Zion with songs and everlasting joy upon their heads: they shall obtain joy and gladness, and sorrow and mourning shall flee away.
Isaiah 35:10 KJV

Let Sorrow do its work, send grief or pain;
Sweet are thy messengers, sweet their refrain.
If they but work in me, more love, O Christ, to thee,
More love to thee, more love to thee.

CALLED TO HELP

Are you called to help others?
Do it with all the strength and
energy that God supplies, so
that God will be glorified.
1 Peter 4:11 TLB

It is one of the lovely things about the Master we serve, that he is so willing to use in his service dwarves as well as giants, and feeble folk as well as champions.

FEBRUARY 18

YOUR WILL

I desire to do your will, O my God;
your law is within my heart.
Psalm 40:8 NIV

It is the will to obey me which makes the union complete between us and which enables me to pour my life and power into those who love me and respond to me continually.

THE WORK OF YOUR HAND

Yet, O Lord, you are our Father.
We are the clay, you are the potter;
we are all the work of your hand
... Oh, look upon us, we pray, for
we are all your people.
Isaiah 64:8-9 NIV

The material was cut and kneaded and shaped as he saw fit, but always the clay lay still upon the wheel, submitting to his every touch, perfectly, unresisting.

FEBRUARY 20

THE MIND CONTROLLED

Those who live in accordance with the Spirit have their minds set on what the Spirit desires ... the mind controlled by the Spirit is life and peace.
Romans 8:5-6 NIV

We are to experience the reign of our Lord and Savior who is Holy Love, completely controlling our whole thought life, and converting our minds into realms of radiant, creative love.

FEBRUARY 21

SAVING OTHERS

This is my commandment, That ye love one another, as I have loved you. Greater love hath no man than this, that a man lay down his life for his friends.
John 15:12-13 KJV

Here on earth we have the opportunity to do what the God of love does all the time, and to learn to abandon ourselves to loving, to giving, to seeking, and to saving others.

FEBRUARY 22

POWER IN PRAYER

*Call unto me, and I will answer thee,
and show thee great and mighty
things, which thou knowest not.*
Jeremiah 33:3 KJV

Many of God's people are longing,
with an ever deepening intensity, for
power in prayer, and seeking to understand how they may experience and practise this greatest possible privilege and
delight.

THE PRISON OF RESENTMENT

Let all bitterness, and wrath, and anger, and clamour, and evil speaking, be put away from you, with all malice: And be ye kind one to another, tenderhearted, forgiving one another.
Ephesians 4:31-32 KJV

There is no prison house so cruel as the prison of resentment and self-pity, and the effect on those who languish long in that bondage is to suffer a progressively destructive influence on character, personality and physical health.

THE HUMBLE

The Lord takes delight in his people;
he crowns the humble with salvation.
Psalm 149:4 TLB

The secret of experiencing true love is to go lower. Pour yourself down. Go lower and lower. Give and give and give, and serve with joyful abandonment.

FEBRUARY 25

NEWNESS OF LIFE

We have been buried with him by baptism into death, so that, just as Christ was raised from the dead by the glory of the Father, so we too might walk in newness of life.
Romans 6:4 NRSV

He begins to pour new wine into new bottles, and a new phase in our Christian and spiritual life begins, a maturing into the heavenly and eternal life.

PERFECT FAITH

For if you had faith even as small as a tiny mustard seed you could say to this mountain, "Move!" and it would go far away. Nothing would be impossible.
Matthew 17:20 TLB

"Faith is certainly a very lovely thing," said the King with a pleased smile. "I can do anything, yes anything, where there is this perfect faith or responsiveness to my will."

FEBRUARY 27

CLAIM THE PROMISES

*Your kingdom is an everlasting
kingdom, and your dominion
endures through all generations ...
You open your hand and satisfy
the desires of every living thing.*
Psalm 145:13, 16 NIV

Claim the great and precious promises
which I have given you, so that you may
become more and more a partaker of my
divine nature of perfect, holy, selfless,
divine love.

FEBRUARY 28

EVERYTHING IS POSSIBLE

*Everything is possible
for him who believes.*
Mark 9:23 NIV

In all the world I have no one but you.
Help me to follow you, even though it
seems impossible. Help me to trust you
as much as I long to love you.

FEBRUARY 29

CHRIST'S AMBASSADORS

*We are therefore Christ's ambassadors,
as though God were making his appeal
through us ... Be reconciled to God.*
2 Corinthians 5:20 NIV

God has chosen us, in Christ Jesus (as
it were, plugged into the life of Christ),
to be transmitters of his life and power
and love to others ... It is God's purpose
that every individual believer in Christ
should become a transmitter.

MARCH

MARCH 1

GOD'S THOUGHTS

Just as the heavens are higher than the earth, so are my ways higher than yours, and my thoughts than yours.
Isaiah 55:9 TLB

How precious God's thoughts are! How far past finding out! How utterly safe it is to trust him if only we are willing to obey and leave all the responsibility to him.

MARCH 2

HIS OWN PURPOSE

Many are the plans in a man's heart, but it is the Lord's purpose that prevails.
Poverbs 19:21 NIV

He has brought me here when I did not want to come, for his own purpose. I, too, will look up into his face and say, "Behold me! I am thy little handmaiden Acceptance-with-Joy."

MARCH 3

HIS SAVING POWER

I am not ashamed of the Good News about Christ. It is God's powerful method of bringing all who believe it to heaven.
Romans 1:16 TLB

Our Lord and Savior Jesus Christ is the actual power house and abiding in him, that is, plugged into him by faith, we transmit his saving power to others.

BY MY SPIRIT

Not by might, nor by power, but by my spirit, says the Lord of hosts.
Zechariah 4:6 NRSV

O Spirit move as thou dost please,
My heart yields at thy word.
Faith hears thee calling from beyond
And doth respond.

MARCH 5

THE GOAL OF GIVING

*Whatever you do, work at it with all
your heart, as working for the Lord,
not for men, since you will receive an
inheritance from the Lord as a reward.
It is the Lord Christ you are serving.*
Colossians 3:23-24 NIV

To be utterly abandoned to the goal of
giving oneself to others, and going down
lower, is the joy and ecstasy of love.

MARCH 6

SHARE HIS SUFFERING

His Holy Spirit speaks to us deep in our hearts, and tells us that we really are God's children. Since we are his children, we will share his treasures – for all God gives to his Son Jesus is now ours too. But if we are to share his glory, we must also share his suffering.
Romans 8:16-17 TLB

It is a well-proved fact that the kingdom of love can come to greater perfection in the heart and minds of those who suffer greatly than under easier circumstances.

THE HAPPY NEWS

How beautiful upon the mountains are the feet of those who bring the happy news of peace and salvation.
Isaiah 52:7 TLB

Love is the constraining power which makes my lovers willing to go all lengths, even to death itself, in order to bring the good news of the love of God to those who have never heard it.

MARCH 8

THE DAY

The work of each builder will become visible, for the Day will disclose it, because it will be revealed with fire, and the fire will test what sort of work each has done.

1 Corinthians 3:13 NRSV

We went on, praying earnestly for revival, that God would sweep away all that was only nominal Christianity, and burn and consume with holy fire all that was false and spurious.

MARCH 9

SUFFERING

I want to know Christ and the power of his resurrection and the fellowship of his sufferings, becoming like him in his death, and so, somehow, to attain to the resurrection from the dead.
Philippians 3:10-11

Why, oh why, must you make Sorrow and Suffering my companions?
– Much-Afraid

MARCH 10

GRANTING OUR REQUESTS

Ask, and it shall be given you; seek, and ye shall find; knock, and it shall be opened unto you: For every one that asketh receiveth; and he that seeketh findeth; and to him that knocketh, it shall be opened.
Matthew 7:7-8 KJV

Not to make our requests known in joyful trust does deprive him of the joy of granting our requests, and it does deprive us of the joy of experiencing his loving, intimate interest in every detail of our lives.

A CHEERFUL GIVER

The one who sows sparingly will also reap sparingly, and the one who sows bountifully will also reap bountifully ... God loves a cheerful giver.
2 Corinthians 9:6-7 NRSV

The poured-out life gives life and power to others. The more love gives, the more it fulfills itself.

MARCH 12

RICHER MEANINGS

*We have not stopped praying for you
and asking God to fill you with the
knowledge of his will through all spiritual wisdom and understanding ...
bearing fruit in every good work,
growing in the knowledge of God.*
Colossians 1:9-10 NIV

After certain experiences of obedience
and acceptance of the will of God ... new
and fuller and richer meanings reveal
themselves in many great passages of
Scripture.

MARCH 13

MEEKNESS

*Blessed are the meek: for they
shall inherit the earth.*
Matthew 5:5 KJV

Meekness is the opposite of self-asser-
tion. It is an attitude of mind which
accepts with joy the will of God, and
bears and forgives all that is done against
it, without resentment.

MARCH 14

THE PLANS I HAVE

"For I know the plans I have for you,"
declares the Lord, "plans to prosper
you and not to harm you, plans to
give you a hope and a future."
Jeremiah 29:11 NIV

It is always safe to trust love's plans, and every lover of mine can sing with fullest assurance, "Surely goodness and mercy shall follow me all the days of my life and I will dwell in the house of the Lord for ever."

MARCH 15

I WILL REFINE THEE

*Grain must be ground to make bread;
so one does not go on threshing it forever ... All this comes from the Lord
Almighty, wonderful in counsel and
magnificent in wisdom.*
Isaiah 28:28-29 NIV

I'll turn my hands upon thy heart,
And purge away the dross,
I will refine thee in my fire
Remake thee at my cross.

MARCH 16

WRONG THINKING

*Resist the devil, and he
will flee from you.*
James 4:7 NIV

We ought to have a great reaction of
horror, disgust, and dread against every
prompting to wrong thinking of any
kind.

THE IMAGINATION

To him who is able to do immeasurably more than all we ask or imagine, according to his power that is at work within us, to him be glory.
Ephesians 3:20-21 NIV

The imagination is the greatest and most creative and God-like function which our Father in heaven has bestowed upon us.

MARCH 18

MY THOUGHT LIFE

*As a man thinketh in
his heart, so is he.*
Proverbs 23:7 KJV

The spirit, or heart of me, is that part
which thinks and wills and chooses, and
therefore it is my thought life which
controls and influences and rules my
whole nature.

YET WILL I TRUST

*Though he slay me, yet
will I trust in him.*
Job 13:15 KJV

She looked at the Shepherd and suddenly knew she could not doubt him,
could not possibly turn back from
following him ... Even if he asked the
impossible, she could not refuse.

MARCH 20

IN THE EVERYDAY LIFE

*Do nothing out of selfish ambition
or vain conceit, but in humility
consider others better than yourselves
... Your attitude should be the same
as that of Christ Jesus.*
Philippians 2:3, 5 NIV

It seems easier to rise to the occasion
when the test is great, perhaps almost
overwhelming, than to live in the
climate of heaven in ordinary and exas-
perating daily circumstances of each one
of us that the reign of love must come.

TO SHARE THE LIFE

*I have raised you up for this very
purpose, that I might show you my
power and that my name might be
proclaimed in all the earth.*
Exodus 9:16 NIV

They could now pour out their lives in
gladdest abandonment, leaping down
with him to the sorrowful, desolate
places below, to share with others the
life which they had received.

MARCH 22

GOD'S GUESTS

*Behold, I stand at the door, and knock:
if any man hear my voice, and open
the door, I will come in to him, and
will sup with him, and he with me.*
Revelation 3:20 KJV

Love's table spread for them,
they may
As God's guests, feast with him.
Their happy faces shine with bliss,
With joy from him and one with his.

MARCH 23

GIVER OF LIFE

*You granted him authority over
all people that he might give eternal life to all those you have given
him. Now this is eternal life: that
they may know you, the only
true God, and Jesus Christ.*
John 17:2-3 NIV

He is the Lord of Love," said she
softly, "the Lord and Giver of Life."

MARCH 24

THE HOLY THINKER

I am he that searches hearts and minds, and I will repay each of you according to your deeds.
Revelation 2:23 NIV

How vitally necessary it must be for our whole thought life to be completely under the control of the Holy Spirit, the holy thinker himself!

THE GOOD SHEPHERD

*I am the good shepherd, and know
my sheep, and am known of mine.
As the Father knoweth me, even so
know I the Father: and I lay down
my life for the sheep.*
John 10:14-15 KJV

Whenever you call for me, I shall
come. This is the word I now leave with
you. Believe it and practice it with joy.
My sheep hear my voice and they follow me.

ONE GLORIOUS PURPOSE

*The path of the just is as a shining
light, which shineth more and
more unto the perfect day.*
Proverbs 4:18 KJV

All the experiences of life are planned
and permitted with one unspeakably glorious purpose in view, that we may follow on to know the Lord, whom to
know is life eternal.

REFUSAL

*They perish because they refused
to love the truth and so be saved.*
2 Thessalonians 2:10 NIV

It is because they have lied to themselves
about you and have persuaded themselves
that you cannot do them good that they
resist you and turn from your help.
– Grace and Glory

MARCH 28

WITH BOLDNESS

Now, Lord, look upon their threats, and grant to your servants to speak your word with all boldness ... They were all filled with the Holy Spirit and spoke the word of God with boldness.
Acts 4:29, 31 NRSV

The Lord's messengers must be prepared to show their colors courageously, or no witness could be given.

MARCH 29

IN YOU I TRUST

To you, O Lord, I lift up my soul;
in you I trust, O my God.
Psalm 25:1 NIV

Much-Afraid, you have such trustful eyes. Trust is one of the most beautiful things in the world.
– The Shepherd

MARCH 30

GOD'S ARMOR

*Put on all of God's armor so that
you will be able to stand safe against
all strategies and tricks of Satan. For
we are not fighting against people
made of flesh and blood, but against
persons without bodies – the evil
rulers of the unseen world.*

Ephesians 6:11-12 TLB

When the kingdom of God becomes
really established in our own thought
realm, then we shall be out of reach of
the evil influences of all the broadcasting stations of the world, the flesh, and
the devil.

THOROUGHLY FURNISHED

All Scripture is given by inspiration of God, and is profitable for doctrine, for reproof, for correction, for instruction in righteousness: That the man of God may be perfect, thoroughly furnished unto all good works.
2 Timothy 3:16-17 KJV

Even the Bible, rich and full as it is of truth from beginning to end, cannot be properly understood except in the light of one's personal experience of Christ himself.

APRIL

APRIL 1

SPRING

For, lo, the winter is past, the rain is over and gone; The flowers appear on the earth; the time of the singing of birds is come, and the voice of the turtle is heard in the land.
Song of Songs 2:11-12 KJV

A long-deferred spring was just loosening everything from the grip of winter, and all the trees were bursting into fairest green.

ACCEPT ONE ANOTHER

*May the God who gives endurance
and encouragement give you a spirit
of unity ... Accept one another,
then, just as Christ accepted you,
in order to bring praise to God.*
Romans 15:5, 7 NIV

For love comes into the heart, not by
trying to force it, but by accepting
people as they are, and bearing all that
they do against you, which is forgiveness. Are you willing for this?

APRIL 3

I WILL FEAR NO EVIL

The Lord is my shepherd, I shall not be in want ... He restores my soul. He guides me in paths of righteousness for his name's sake. Even though I walk through the valley of the shadow of death, I will fear no evil, for you are with me.
Psalm 23:1, 3-4 NIV

No evil which is done to us can harm us ultimately, for it will be compensated for by God himself.

APRIL 4

HIS VOICE

He calls his own sheep by name and leads them out ... His sheep follow him because they know his voice.
John 10:3-4 NIV

Whenever you are willing to obey me, Much-Afraid, and to follow the path of my choice, you will always be able to hear and recognize my voice, and when you hear it you must always obey.

APRIL 5

HIS DWELLING PLACE

I am crucified with Christ: nevertheless I live; yet not I, but Christ liveth in me: and the life which I now live in the flesh I live by the faith of the Son of God, who loved me, and gave himself for me.
Galatians 2:20 KJV

We are so completely transformed through the renewing of our minds that we literally become new creatures in whom the Holy Spirit of love makes his dwelling place, just as he dwelt in our Lord and Savior.

THINGS HE HAS DONE

Trust the Lord and sincerely worship him; think of all the tremendous things he has done for you.
1 Samuel 12:24 TLB

When they see what you have done for me, when they see Peace and Joy, I do think in the end they will want you to help them too.

MEETING OUR NEEDS

He will supply all your needs from his riches in glory, because of what Christ Jesus has done for us.
Philippians 4:19 TLB

God always has enough ready and waiting to meet our needs, no matter what they may be, and no matter how impossible the circumstances look.

APRIL 8

FREELY GIVE

Freely you have received, freely give.
Matthew 10:8 NIV

This is the law by which we live –
It is so sweet to give and give.

THE SIN OF THE WORLD

He himself bore our sins in his body
on the cross, so that, free from sins,
we might life for righteousness; by
his wounds you have been healed.
1 Peter 2:24 NRSV

Not just once only, for six hours when Jesus the Incarnate Word hung upon the cross and died a physical death, did God bear the sin of the world, but from the first moment of man's sinning, his cross began.

THE CROSS

May I never boast except in the cross of our Lord Jesus Christ, through which the world has been crucified to me, and I to the world.
Galatians 6:14 NIV

The Cross does stand at the very heart and center of the Christian life – the cross of our Lord and Savior Jesus Christ, by which he achieved our deliverance from the bondage of sin and self-love and opens to us the means of sharing his own life.

ETERNAL LIFE

And this is the testimony: God gave us eternal life, and this life is in his Son. Whoever has the Son has life; whoever does not have the Son of God does not have life.
1 John 5:11-12 NRSV

"I have been to the Kingdom of Love," said she, "and have died to the old loveless life which is death. And Love has been planted in my heart and lives there. Love is eternal. The Life that is love can never die. It is eternal life."

REST FOR YOUR SOULS

Stand at the crossroads and look; ask for the ancient paths, ask where the good way is, and walk in it, and you will find rest for you souls.
Jeremiah 6:16 NIV

You are longing beyond all words to be restored and to be in communion with the Savior again, and you can find no rest or peace until you are. That is a sure sign that his Spirit is even now working in you.

ALWAYS SAFE

A man is a fool to trust himself! But those who use God's wisdom are safe.
Proverbs 28:26 TLB

Remember also that it is always safe to obey my voice, even if it seems to call you to paths which look impossible or even crazy.

AN INSTRUMENT

*If a man cleanses himself ... he will
be an instrument for noble purposes,
made holy, useful to the Master and
prepared to do any good work.*
2 Timothy 2:21 NIV

We allow the Holy Spirit to use our
bodies to perform visible acts of love
and compassion and kindness and suc-
cour and justice and integrity and righteousness, etc., in a thousand practical and
visible ways, which reveal the love and
will of God.

TWO MASTERS

Neither you nor anyone else can serve two masters. You will hate one and show loyalty to the other, or else the other way around – you will be enthusiastic about one and despise the other. You cannot serve both God and money.
Luke 16:13 TLB

One cannot love God and wealth too," said the Shepherd. "It simply cannot be done."

APRIL 16

THE JUDGE

The Lord reigns forever; he has established his throne for judgement. He will judge the world in righteousness.
Psalm 9:7-8 NIV

The judge of your whole life – of how you have lived and how you have used this body which was lent you, and the things you possessed here on earth. He will judge as to whether you have obeyed the law of love.

APRIL 17

A FRESH NEWNESS

Don't copy the behavior and customs of this world, but be a new and different person with a fresh newness in all you do and think.
Romans 12:2 TLB

When we are in him so that his life courses through us, then the Holy Spirit transforms us "by the renewing of our minds" and we become transmitters to others.

APRIL 18

GOD'S GRACE

*I became a servant of this gospel
by the gift of God's grace given me
through the work of his power.*
Ephesians 3:7 NIV

It is only up on the High Places of Love
that anyone can receive the power to
pour themselves down in an utter aban
donment of self-giving.

THE UNIVERSE OF LOVE

*Therefore my heart is glad and my
tongue rejoices ... You have made
known to me the paths of life; you will
fill me with joy in your presence.*
Acts 2:26, 28 NIV

The King of Love seemed to by saying
with a glad laugh, "Now you have become part of a new universe altogether,
the universe of love. And all you have
to do now is to begin to explore it, and
to revel in it."

APRIL 20

LISTEN TO HIS VOICE

*Choose life, so that you and
your children may live and that you
may love the Lord your God, listen
to his voice, and hold fast to him.
For the Lord is your life.*
Deuteronomy 30:19-20 NIV

The least child of God can hear in the
same way, and be sure that it is the voice
of God speaking to him, as any holy man
of old.

THE VOICE OF THE LORD

I heard the voice of the Lord,
saying, Whom shall I send,
and who will go for us? Then
said I, Here am I; send me.
Isaiah 6:8 KJV

I need a voice to speak for me, to persuade them to let me help them.

APRIL 22

THE FOOLISH WEAK

Think of what you were when you were called. Not many of you were wise by human standards; not many were influential; not many were of noble birth. But God chose the foolish things of the world to shame the wise; God chose the weak things of the world to shame the strong.
1 Corinthians 1:26-27 NIV

How glorious are the foolish weak
By God made greatly strong:
So strong they take the conqueror's
crown,
. And turn the whole world upside
down.

HE IS THE TRUTH

I am the way, and the truth, and the life. No one comes to the Father, except through me. If you know me, you will know my Father also. From now on you do know him and have seen him.
John 14:6-7 NRSV

He is the truth, full of truth. Only as we follow him in obedience can we come to know more and more of truth.

APRIL 24

SEEK THE LORD

*Seek the Lord while you can find him.
Call upon him now while he is near.
Let men cast off their wicked deeds ...
Let them turn to the Lord that he may
have mercy upon them, and to our
God, for he will abundantly pardon!*
Isaiah 55:6-7

He has only waited with the utmost
love and patience until the time should
come when you would be ready at last
to listen to him and to seek his help.

JOY COMETH

*For his anger endureth but a
moment; in his favour is life:
weeping may endure for a night,
by joy cometh in the morning.*
Psalm 30:5 KJV

When the sun thus shone on the wild
wastes of waters it seemed as though all
their sorrows had been swallowed up in
joy, and then she would whisper ...
"When he hath tried me, I will come
forth as gold. Weeping may endure for
a night, but joy cometh in the morning."

APRIL 26

GLAD FORGIVENESS

*He has rescued us from the
power of darkness and transferred
us into the kingdom of his beloved
Son, in whom we have redemption,
the forgiveness of sins.*
Colossians 1:13-14 NRSV

The habit of glad forgiveness, through
willingness to bear the wrong and to
atone as far as possible, is an inescapable
and glorious law in the kingdom of love.

APRIL 27

LOWLY SPIRIT

A man's pride brings him low, but a
man of lowly spirit gains honor.
Proverbs 29:23 NIV

From the heights we leap and flow
To the valleys down below.
Always answering the call,
To the lowest place of all.
Sweetest urge and sweetest pain,
To go low and rise again.

REJOICE

Always be full of joy in the Lord; I say it again, rejoice!
Philippians 4:4 TLB

The secret of victorious Christian living and creative power is to go through each day praising God for everything: the bad things as well as the good.

FORSAKEN

Yet I hold this against you: You have forsaken your first love
Revelation 2:4 NIV

The real cause of disunity and weakness in the Church is through having left the first center of love and loyalty, namely, our Lord himself, who is Savior and King and Leader.

KEEP ON PRAYING

*Always be joyful. Always keep
on praying. No matter what
happens, always be thankful,
for this is God's will for you.*
1 Thessalonians 5:16-18 TLB

We pray without ceasing when all our
thoughts are under the control of the
Holy Spirit.

MAY

MAY 1

SLAVES TO GOD

*You have been set free from sin
and have become slaves to God.*
Romans 6:22 NIV

Owned thy claims upon me,
thou my Master only,
I thy slave forever,
Nothing henceforth mine.

A HARVEST OF RIGHTEOUSNESS

God disciplines us for our good, that we may share in his holiness. No discipline seems pleasant at the time, but painful. Later on, however, it produces a harvest of righteousness and peace ...
Hebrews 12:10-11 NIV

Love, which is the most beautiful and most gentle passion, can and must be at the same time the most terrible – terrible in what it is willing to endure itself in order to secure the blessing and happiness and perfection of the beloved.

THE KINGDOM OF LOVE

My people have been lost sheep ...
They wandered over mountain and
hill and forgot their own resting place.
Jeremiah 50:6 NIV

I cannot bear to think of their wretched condition while I live up here in the Kingdom of Love.

NONE WILL BE LOST

*If a man owns a hundred sheep,
and one of them wanders away,
will he not leave the ninety-nine on
the hill and go look for the one? ...
In the same way your Father in
heaven is not willing that any
of these little ones be lost.*
Matthew 18:12, 14 NIV

The one thing we cannot do, we who
have tasted of his love and grace, and
been lifted out of the darkness, is to sit
back comfortably and leave him alone
in the task of searching for the lost.

THE FLOOD-TIDE OF LOVE

Happy are those who long to be just and good, for they shall be completely satisfied.
Matthew 5:6 TLB

"O my Lord," she cried, "I thank thee for leading me here. Behold me, here I am, empty as was this little cove, but waiting thy time to be filled to the brim with the flood-tide of Love."

TEMPTATIONS

*For we have not a high priest who
is unable to sympathize with our
weaknesses, but we have one who
in every respect has been tested
as we are, yet without sin.*
Hebrews 4:15 NRSV

He faced every temptation possible to
human beings, and he showed that the
only way to overcome these temptations
was to allow the Holy Spirit of love to
control his thoughts and his feelings and
to show him how to react.

THE UNITY OF
THE SPIRIT

*Be patient, bearing with one
another in love. Make every effort
to keep the unity of the Spirit
through the bond of peace.*
Ephesians 4:2-3 NIV

The way to unity of doctrine is not by
definitions, but by practicing the unity
of the Spirit, in the bonds of love, on
the way to knowing the full truth, concerning Jesus.

MAY 8

THE TREE OF LOVE

*Stand firm in the faith; be
men of courage; be strong.
Do everything in love.*
1 Corinthians 16:13-14 NIV

Every inner response of the human
heart to Love and every conquest over
self-love is a new flower on the tree of
Love.

AN INESCAPABLE CHALLENGE

In everything set them an example by doing what is good. In your teaching show integrity, seriousness and soundness of speech that cannot be condemned.
Titus 2:7-8 NIV

The faith and life of our parents presented us with an inescapable challenge, and no child of theirs could easily drift into unbelief, or be unaffected by the things that are true and eternal.

EVIL THOUGHTS

*Let the wicked forsake his way, and
the unrighteous man his thoughts,
and let him return unto the Lord ...
For my thoughts are not your
thoughts, and my ways are not
your ways, saith the Lord.*
Isaiah 55:7-8 KJV

If we are going to be God's transmitters, our minds must be shut and
garrisoned against every approach of evil
thought waves.

LOVE THEM

*Anyone who claims to be in
the light but hates his brother is
still in darkness. Whoever loves
his brother lives in the light.*
1 John 2:9-10 NIV

As my disciple, there is, of course, no
question of your hating anyone. You will
love them as I love them.

A CREATIVE PRINCIPLE

Anyone whom you forgive, I also forgive. What I have forgiven, if I have forgiven anything, has been for your sake in the presence of Christ.
2 Corintians 2:10 NRSV

For forgiveness is a gloriously creative principle, and can generate in us (as it did, of course, in a unique way in our Lord) a saving and liberating power which can reach and change others.

SHOW MERCY

*Be merciful to those who doubt;
snatch others from the fire and save
them; to others show mercy.*
Jude 22:23 NIV

She had thought of them only as horrible enemies, but now she realized that they were just miserable beings such as she had been herself.

MAY 14

HIS FOLLOWERS

*If any want to become my followers,
let them deny themselves and take
up their cross and follow me. For
those who want to save their life
will lose it, and those who lose
their life for my sake, and for the
sake of the gospel, will save it.*
Mark 8:34-35 NRSV

He denied himself and took up his
cross daily, and this was the principle he
commanded his followers.

UNFAILING LOVE

*"Though the mountains be shaken and
the hills be removed, yet my unfailing
love for you will not be shaken nor my
covenant of peace be removed," says
the Lord, who has compassion on you.*
Isaiah 54:10 NIV

Self-Pity would chime in ... "Can you
really believe when he acts toward you
like this that he loves you and has your
real good at heart? How can that be possible?"

THE LOVE OF CHRIST

We love because he first loved us.
1 John 4:19 NRSV

At my conversion the overwhelming glory and wonder of the Love of Christ himself, the King of Love, broke into my wretched, cold little heart with amazingly transforming power, and for the first time I felt what it was to love him.

THE FAIREST BEAUTIES

*He will not forget your work
and the love you have shown him
as you have helped his people
and continue to help them.*
Hebrews 6:10 NIV

All the fairest beauties in the human soul, its greatest victories, and its most splendid achievements are always those which no one else knows anything about.

MAY 18

THE SPIRIT OF THE LORD

*As the Spirit of the Lord
works within us, we become
more and more like him.*
2 Corinthians 3:18 TLB

To purify his loved – 'tis fire,
A holy fire to burn.
For he must fully perfect thee
Till in thy likeness all may see
The beauty of thy Lord.

MAY 19

"I AM READY"

*May the God of peace ... equip you
with every good thing for doing his
will, and may he work in us what is
pleasing to him, through Jesus Christ.*
Hebrews 13:20-21 NIV

Whenever we say truly from the heart,
"I am ready" for God's will whatever it
is, we shall certainly experience his faithfulness and providential dealings in ways
which to other people will often appear
extraordinary.

MAY 20

IN MY NAME

Whatsoever ye shall ask in my name that will I do, that the Father may be glorified in the Son. If ye shall ask any thing in my name, I will do it.
John 14:13-14 KJV

Only when we know and share in desires of our Lord Jesus Christ, can we really pray in his name, and not in our own.

MAY 21

FAITHFUL IS HE

*I pray God your whole spirit and
soul and body be preserved blameless unto the coming of our Lord
Jesus Christ. Faithful is he that
calleth you, who also will do it.*
1 Thessalonians 5:23-24 KJV

How truly and joyfully I can testify
as I look back over my path of life "faithful is he that calleth you, who also will
do it."

MAY 22

SALVATION

*Ye are sanctified, but ye are justified
in the name of the Lord Jesus, and
by the Spirit of our God.*
1 Corinthians 6:11 KJV

We are in need of salvation, a deliverance and cleansing and transforming salvation, greater and more important than anything we have understood hitherto.

THE SACRIFICES OF GOD

*Create in me a pure heart, O God,
and renew a steadfast spirit within me
... The sacrifices of God are a broken
spirit; a broken and contrite heart,
O God, you will not despise.*
Psalm 51:10, 17 NIV

We may be quite sure that the Creator, our Lord Jesus Christ, does not allow any breaking and shattering process in our lives without design.

PATIENT IN AFFLICTION

Keep your spiritual fervor, serving the Lord. Be joyful in hope, patient in affliction, faithful in prayer.
Romans 12:11-12 NIV

When you wear the weed of impatience in your heart instead of the flower Acceptance-with-Joy, you will always find your enemies get an advantage over you.

THE LOWLY SERVICE

*Now that I, your Lord and Teacher,
have washed your feet, you also
should wash one another's feet. I
have set you an example that you
should do as I have done for you.*
John 13:14-15 NIV

Surely to wash one another's feet is to
cleanse them completely in our
thoughts, and to find through the lowly
but adventurous service of love a means
of helping them.

A LOVING HAND

*Carry each other's burdens, and in this
way you will fulfill the law of Christ.*
Galatians 6:2 NIV

There broke over her heart an agonizing flood of sorrow. She longed for
fellowship again, for the touch of one
really loving hand, for the sound of one
really friendly voice.

A GENTLE SPIRIT

Let your adornment be the inner self with the lasting beauty of a gentle and quiet spirit, which is very precious in God's sight.
1 Peter 3:4 NRSV

Thy gentleness hath made me great,
And I would gentle be ...
'Tis meekness wins, not force nor might,
Lord, teach this grace to me.
Though others should resist my love,
I may be gentle as a dove.

MAY 28

BE UNITED WITH HIM

If we have been united with him like this in his death, we will certainly also be united with him in his resurrection ... Now if we died with Christ, we believe we will also live with him.
Romans 6:5, 8 NIV

Accept and bear and obey the Law of Love, and nothing will be able to cripple your hind's feet or to separate you from me. This is the secret of the High Places.

HOLY LOVE

*He will baptize you with the
Holy Spirit and with fire.*
Matthew 3:11 NRSV

Lord, baptize me with holy love ... I
pray to be baptized into thyself, thou
who art love – that I may be set down in
love, and be filled with love, and be kept
in love the whole time.

MAY 30

HUMBLE YOURSELF

*When you realize your worthlessness
before the Lord, he will lift you up,
encourage and help you.*
James 4:10 TLB

Humble yourself, and you will find
that Love is spreading a carpet of flowers beneath your feet.

BECOME LIKE LITTLE CHILDREN

*Unless you change and become
like little children, you will never
enter the kingdom of heaven.
Therefore, whoever humbles
himself like this child is the greatest in the kingdom of heaven.*
Matthew 18:3-4 NIV

The great principle of the hearing heart
is that we become as little children, utterly dependent and always ready to obey
... Learning to hear and obey is the most
vital thing in Christian experience.

JUNE

OBEY HIS WORDS

I have promised to obey your words. I have sought your face with all my heart; be gracious to me according to your promise.
Psalm 119:57-58 NIV

Learning to hear and to understand and to obey is the most vital thing in Christian experience.

JUNE 2

THE HEAVENLY PLACES

*Blessed be the God and Father of our
Lord Jesus Christ, who has blessed us
in Christ with every spiritual blessing
in the heavenly places, just as he
chose us in Christ before the founda-
tion of the world to be holy and
blameless before him in love.*
Ephesians 1:3-4 NRSV

It is through the door of death that we
pass out from the prison of self and can
swoop up into the glorious joy and lib-
erty of the heavenly places.

PATHS OF SORROW

They will be his people, and God himself will be with them and be their God. He will wipe every tear from their eyes. There will be no more death or mourning or crying or pain.
Revelation 21:3-4 NIV

The heart knoweth its own sorrow and there are times when it is comforting to think that our tears are put in a bottle and not one of them forgotten by the one who leads us in paths of sorrow.

JUNE 4

GIVING YOURSELF

*Each man will be like a shelter from
the wind and a refuge from the
storm, like streams of water in the
desert and the shadow of a great rock
in a thirsty land ... till the Spirit is
poured on us from on high, and the
desert becomes a fertile field.*
Isaiah 32:2, 15 NIV

To love is to give oneself, to lay down
one's self, to share oneself with others,
as the grass gives itself to the cattle, and
the water to the thirsty land, and as the
sun gives its light and warmth freely to
good and bad alike.

JUNE 5

OVERCOME EVIL
WITH GOOD

*Do not be overcome by evil, but
overcome evil with good.*
Romans 12:21 NRSV

That is the only really satisfactory way
of dealing with evil, not simply binding
it so that it cannot work harm, but whenever possible overcoming it with good.

THE JOY OF HEAVEN

*At his tabernacle will I sacrifice
with shouts of joy; I will sing and
make music to the Lord ... My
heart says of you, "Seek his face!"
Your face, Lord, I will seek.*
Psalm 27:6, 7 NIV

Where love reigns, the very joy of
heaven itself is felt.

YOUR GENTLENESS

*Let your gentleness be evident
to all. The Lord is near.*
Philippians 4:5 NIV

She whispered to herself most grate-
fully, "His gentleness hath made me
great." and "Oh, how I long to be
anointed with the same gentleness to-
wards others!"

LOVE IS A LIFE

But when the kindness and love of God our Savior appeared ... he saved us through the washing of rebirth and renewal by the Holy Spirit, whom he poured out on us generously through Jesus Christ our Savior.
Titus 3:4-6 NIV

Love is a life which must flood into our whole being, into the deepest depths and last abyss of our being, filling and transforming the whole world or realm of our personality.

COMMIT YOUR WAY

Commit your way to the Lord:
trust in him and he will do this:
He will make your righteousness
shine like the dawn.
Psalm 37:5-6 NIV

"I am here," said Much-Afraid, still kneeling at his feet, "and I will go with you anywhere."

JUNE 10

A HEARING HEART

*The man who looks intently into the
perfect law that gives freedom, and
continues to do this, not forgetting
what he has heard, but doing it – he
will be blessed in what he does.*
James 1:25 NIV

A hearing heart depends upon an utter
willingness to obey, the whole time, in
tiny details as well as big ones. In Hebrew, an "obedient heart" is the same
word as a "hearing heart."

JUNE 11

YOUR CHOICE

*Choose you this day whom ye
will serve ... but as for me and my
house, we will serve the Lord.*
Joshua 24:15 KJV

A human spirit is indeed a capacity to
love and to respond to love and according to what it chooses or wills to love
so will its woe or blessedness be.

JUNE 12

NEW ENRICHMENT

*Every good and perfect gift is
from above, and cometh down
from the Father of lights, with
whom is no variableness,
neither shadow of turning.*
James 1:17 KJV

Don't try to hold on to anything in this
life, but willingly let go, in order to be
able to receive new enrichment from the
Lord.

LIKE A SHEPHERD

He shall feed his flock like a shepherd:
he shall gather the lambs with his arm,
and carry them in his bosom, and shall
gently lead those that are with young.
Isaiah 40:11 KJV

I tell you now with all my heart that
you are my Shepherd whose voice I love
to hear and obey, and that it is my joy
to follow you. You choose, my Lord,
and I will obey.

JUNE 14

THE GOOD NEWS

*Go into all the world and preach the
Good News to everyone, everywhere.*
Mark 16:15 TLB

Like royal banners bright, unfurled,
Now I go forth, my Lord,
Strong through thy mighty word,
To stake out claims around the world.

JUNE 15

RECEIVE THE LORD

*To all who received him, he gave the
right to become children of God.*
John 1:12 TLB

Forth from the love of God he came,
And seeks thine empty heart.
Receive this Lord from heaven above,
In thee to live his life of love.

JUNE 16

ACCEPTANCE

*My soul finds rest in God alone; my
salvation comes from him. He alone is
my rock and my salvation; he is my
fortress, I will never be shaken.*
Psalm 62:1-2 NIV

In acceptance lieth peace,
O my heart be still;
Let thy restless worries cease
And accept his will.

JUNE 17

HIS FAITHFUL ONES

*Turn from evil and do good; then
you will dwell in the land forever.
For the Lord loves the just and will
not forsake his faithful ones.*
Psalm 37:27-28 NIV

Therefore I begin to think, my Lord,
you purposely allow us to be brought
into contact with the bad and evil things
that you want changed. Perhaps that is
the very reason why we are here in this
world.

JUNE 18

HIS PERFECT WORK

The very God of peace sanctify you wholly; and I pray God your whole spirit and soul and body be preserved blameless unto the coming of our Lord Jesus Christ. Faithful is he that calleth you, who also will do it.
1 Thessalonians 5:23-24 KJV

Surely that is what our Lord's own prayers are, creative thinking about each one of us; seeing us with all our beset-ting sins, weaknesses, ugly blemishes completely removed, and the whole per-sonality as it will be when his perfect work in us is finished.

THE SHEPHERD CALLED

We are the people of his pasture, the flock under his care. Today, if you hear his voice, do not harden your hearts.
Psalm 95:7-8 NIV

The Shepherd came and called me as he promised, but I didn't go to him or give any answer.

"ABBA, FATHER."

Those who are led by the Spirit of God are sons of God. For you did not receive a spirit that makes you a slave again to fear, but you received the Spirit of sonship. And by him we cry, "Abba, Father."
Romans 8:14-15 NIV

As he is God, and we are his beloved children, our prayer will take the form of a conversation in which we not only speak to him, but also listen to him and learn of him.

THE FRUIT OF THE SPIRIT

The fruit of the Spirit is love, joy, peace, patience, kindness, goodness, faithfulness, gentleness and self-control ... Those who belong to Christ Jesus have crucified the sinful nature ... Since we live by the Spirit, let us keep in step with the Spirit.
Galatians 5:22-25 NIV

Love must rule in the whole realm of or individual personality, the whole world of our being must be under his control. Love must be king of the vast realms of our minds, that is to say of our complete thought life.

A GLORIOUS REALIZATION

So we say with confidence, "The Lord is my helper; I will not be afraid."
Hebrews 13:6 NIV

The Lord Jesus is able, in such time of crisis, to overcome our natural fears and give such a glorious realization of his presence that everything else is swallowed up.

A WELL-WATERED GARDEN

He will satisfy your needs in a sun-scorched land and will strengthen your frame. You will be like a well-watered garden, like a spring whose waters never fail.
Isaiah 58:11 NIV

I am afraid there is nothing much in the garden of my heart as yet, Shepherd, but all that there is, is yours to do with as you please.

JUNE 24

BE AT REST

Be at rest once more, O my soul,
for the Lord has been good to you.
For you, O Lord, have delivered my
soul from death, my eyes from tears,
and my feet from stumbling, that I
may walk before the Lord.
Psalm 116:8-9 NIV

Joy is sorrow accepted and overcome,
and peace comes into being through the
acceptance of fear and anxiety and rest-
lessness and uncertainty and insecurity.

JUNE 25

HE GIVETH GRACE

But he giveth more grace. Wherefore he saith, God resisteth the proud, but giveth grace to the humble. Submit yourselves therefore to God.
James 4:6-7 KJV

It was this gentle movement of submissiveness, combined with perfect balance and graceful motion, which produced the cadences of music sounding all over the mountainside.

JUNE 26

FAITHFULNESS

*Let us hold fast the confession
of our hope without wavering, for
he who promised is faithful.*
Hebrews 10:23 NRSV

Faith is being willing to test the faithfulness of God ... It generally means
openly taking some sort of risk and
being willing to look a fool before
others.

DARKNESS INTO LIGHT

*The Lord turns my darkness into
light ... It is God who arms me with
strength and makes my way perfect.*
2 Samuel 22:29, 33 NIV

Every circumstance in life, no matter
how crooked and distorted and ugly it
appears to be, if it is reacted to in love
and forgiveness and obedience to your
will can be transformed.

JUNE 28

ABOUND IN LOVE

*And the Lord make you to increase
and abound in love one toward
another, and toward all men.*
1 Thessalonians 3:12 KJV

Love must express itself, and seeks for
every opportunity to do so.

GOD SHALL REJOICE

*As the bridegroom rejoiceth
over the bride, so shall thy
God rejoice over thee.*
Isaiah 62:5 KJV

He looketh through my window,
And beckoneth unto me.
"Rise up, my love, my fair one,
And come away with me."

I AM HIS

He brought me to the banqueting house, and his banner over me was love ... My beloved is mine, and I am his.
Song of Solomon 2:4, 16 KJV

My bonds are very, very strong.
I never can go free:
To Holy Love I now belong.
An he belongs to me.

JULY

LOVE YOUR NEIGHBOUR

The commandments ... are summed up in this one rule: "Love your neighbor as yourself." Love does no harm to its neighbor. Therefore love is the fulfillment of the law.
Romans 13:9-10 NIV

Love which worketh no ill to her neighbor is the fulfillment of the whole law on which the universe is founded.

JULY 2

WE WERE HEALED

*He was wounded and bruised for
our sins. He was beaten that we
might have peace; he was lashed –
and we were healed!*
Isaiah 53:5 TLB

He was wounded and has been wounded
for our transgressions all along. From
the moment of the first sin it began to
be true.

JULY 3

LIVE AGAIN

*If the many died by the trespass
of the one man, ... how much more
will those who receive God's abundant
provision of grace and of the gift of
righteousness reign in life through
the one man, Jesus Christ.*
Romans 5:15, 17 NIV

By Adam came all sin and pain.
In Christ shall all men live again.
Behold our God and Savior thus!
See what his Love will do for us.

JULY 4

DO NOT FORGET

Bless the Lord, O my soul, and do not forget all his benefits – who forgives all your iniquity, who heals all your diseases, who redeems your life from the Pit, who crowns you with steadfast love and mercy.
Psalm 103:2-4 NRSV

This world and this earthly life are so arranged that sooner or later every single human soul must realize he is nothing but is absolutely dependent upon me.

JULY 5

GOD LOVES THE WORLD

God loved the world so much that he gave his only Son so that anyone who believes in him shall not perish but have eternal life.
John 3:16 TLB

I began to realize in an absolutely new way how God loves the world, that is to say all these infinitely diverse peoples of the world; his passionate, absorbed interest in everything that goes on, above all, in every individual who lives on this planet.

A NEW THOUGHT LIFE

Thy word have I hid in mine heart,
that I might not sin against thee.
Psalm 119:11 KJV

Our greatest need is to begin a completely new kind of thought life, for there is the very heart and center of our problem. It is there that the seeds of sin begin.

JULY 7

CALL FOR HELP

I lift up my eyes to the hills – from where will my help come? My help comes from the Lord, who made heaven and earth.
Psalm 121:1-2 NRSV

Much-Afraid, you know where your help lies. Call for help.

HIS TASK WITHIN YOU

God who began the good work within you will keep right on helping you grow in his grace until his task within you is finally finished on that day when Jesus Christ returns.
Philippians 1:6 TLB

The new spiritual life of Christ develops slowly and only gradually changes the old temperament and character.

IN GOD I TRUST

When I am afraid, I will trust in you. In God, whose word I praise, in God I trust; I will not be afraid.
Psalm 56:3-4 NIV

The Prince of Love is "of very tender compassions to them that are afraid."

JULY 10

A GIFT FROM GOD

You have been saved through trusting Christ. And even trusting is not of yourselves; it too is a gift from God.
Ephesians 2:8 TLB

Faith is one of God's good gifts. We do not have to labor to try and produce it ourselves. To every poor slave of self who really desires it, is given the power to respond in obedience to our Lord and Savior Jesus Christ.

JULY 11

A CHOSEN GENERATION

But ye are a chosen generation, a royal priesthood, an holy nation, a peculiar people; that ye should show forth the praises of him who hath called you out of darkness into his marvellous light.
1 Peter 2:9 KJV

You always treated me as though I were a queen already and not wretched little Much-Afraid.

THE WEDDING OF THE LAMB

For the wedding of the Lamb has come, and his bride has made herself ready. Fine linen, bright and clean, was given her to wear. [Fine linen stands for the righteous acts of the saints.]
Revelation 19:7-8 NIV

Goodness is such a lovely thing!
'Tis Love's own bridal dress
The wedding garment from our King
Is spotless righteousness.

RECONCILIATION

God was reconciling the world to himself in Christ, not counting men's sins against them. And he has committed to us the message of reconciliation. We are therefore Christ's ambassadors, as though God were making his appeal through us.
2 Corinthians 5:19-20 NIV

Meditating on God's Word, and longing for others to understand it too, is part of the broadcasting to which we are called.

GO WITH ME

If you make the Most High your dwelling – even the Lord, who is my refuge – then no harm will befall you ... For he will command his angels concerning you to guard you in all your ways.
Psalm 91:9-11 NIV

If you will go with me, and face whatever discomfort and weariness there may be on this trip, I promise you that the car will not break down, that you will not get malaria or typhoid, and you will not be shot, nor hurt, nor molested in any way.

JULY 15

A CROSS OF SUFFERING

*All we like sheep have gone astray;
we have turned every one to his own
way; and the Lord hath laid on him
the iniquity of us all.*
Isaiah 53:6 KJV

Ever since the first sin, the love of God
has been, as it were, upon a cross of
suffering.

JULY 16

GOD CHOSE YOU

*From the beginning God chose
you to be saved through the
sanctifying work of the Spirit
and through belief in the truth.*
2 Thessalonians 2:13 NIV

It is the message of the living Savior,
and the leading into personal contact
with him, which saves and transforms
men and women, and triumphs over the
powers of evil in the world.

JULY 17

THE NEW SELF

You have taken off your old self with its practices and have put on the new self, which is being renewed in knowledge in the image of its creator.
Colossians 3:9-10 NIV

You, my Lord, never regarded me as I actually was, lame and weak and crooked and cowardly. You saw me as I would be when you had done what you promised and had brought me to the High Places.

IT WAS VERY GOOD

*And God saw every thing that he had
made, and, behold, it was very good.*
Genesis 1:31 KJV

Judging by the way he has created things
God must have an intense love for, and
interest in, diversity ... Every single
thing he has made differs from everything else. There is not a single blade of
grass exactly like another, nor snow-
flake.

A STREAM OF COURAGE

You do not lack any spiritual gift as you eagerly wait for our Lord Jesus Christ to be revealed. He will keep you strong to the end, so that you will be blameless on the day of Jesus Christ.
1 Corinthians 1:7-8 NIV

Much-Afraid felt as though a strong and exhilarating cordial had been poured into her heart and that a stream of courage and strength was flowing into her from his presence.

UNDER THE CONTROL

*Let not my heart be drawn
to evil ... But my eyes are fixed
on you, O Sovereign Lord.*
Psalm 141:4, 8 NIV

We need to learn the lovely transforming secret of a thought life brought completely and unbrokenly under the control of the Holy Spirit of Love.

JULY 21

THY ROYAL HOUSE

*Surely goodness and mercy
shall follow me all the days of
my life: and I will dwell in the
house of the Lord for ever.*
Psalm 23:6 KJV

Draw me – I will run after thee.
Thou art my heart's one choice.
Oh, bring me to thy royal house,
To dwell there and rejoice.

THEIR UNBELIEF

*He could there do no mighty work ...
and he marvelled at their unbelief.*
Mark 6:5-6 KJV

An evil heart of unbelief consists in a
hardening of our will against God's will,
simply because we do not like what he
has chosen for us, but want our own will
to be done.

THIS IS THE WAY

*If you leave God's paths and go astray,
you will hear a Voice behind you say,
"No, this is the way; walk here."*
Isaiah 30:21 TLB

He does often cause us to walk in
darkness, having no light at all on the
extraordinary path by which he is leading us, but then his precious assurance
is, "What I do thou knowest not now,
but thou shalt know hereafter."

WORTHY IS THE LAMB

*Worthy is the Lamb that was slain
to receive power, and riches, and
wisdom, and strength, and honour,
and glory, and blessing.*
Revelation 5:12 KJV

She looked into his face and put her
hand into his nail-pierced hand, close to
the wound in his side through which his
very life had been poured forth for all
mankind.

OPEN MY EYES

*Open my eyes that I may see
wonderful things in your law ...
Your statutes are my delight;
they are my counselors.*
Psalm 119:18, 24 NIV

It is not that the teaching in the Bible is gradually unfolding revelation, but that we only come to understand it gradually ourselves, just as a child's understanding gradually develops.

JULY 26

SLAVES TO SIN

*Our old self was crucified with him
so that the body of sin might be
done away with, that we should
no longer be slaves to sin ... If
we died with Christ, we believe
that we will also live with him.*
Romans 6:6, 8 NIV

Love will bear and will forgive.
Love will suffer long.
Die to self that she may live.
Triumph over wrong.

JULY 27

FORGIVE WITHOUT BITTERNESS

"Lord, how many times shall I forgive my brother when he sins against me? Up to seven times?" Jesus answered, "I tell you, not seven times, but seventy-seven times."
Matthew 18:21-22 NIV

I learned that I must bear all that others were allowed to do against me and to forgive with no trace of bitterness.

SHOUT WITH JOY

Shout with joy before the Lord,
O earth! Obey him gladly; come
before him, singing with joy.
Psalm 100:1-2 TLB

Find the form which makes it most
easy and natural and joyful to express
(your) praise and love and worship, and
then gladly use that way, and rejoice in
the countless different forms through
which God's other children find the
same blessing.

JULY 29

THE GOOD NEWS

If, when we were God's enemies we were reconciled to him through the death of his Son, how much more, having been reconciled, shall we be saved through his life!
Romans 5:10 NIV

The real good news is the revelation of God conquering sin and bringing life to us, and working with transforming power in the hearts of those who have responded to the revelation made; and conscious of his life risen in us.

JULY 30

THE THRONE ROOM

They are darkened in their under-standing and separated from the life of God because of the ignorance that is in them due to the hardening of their hearts.
Ephesians 4:18 NIV

A hardening of our hearts means a resistance of our wills, for the heart is the throne room, the innermost place of control. And in the heart, either self-will is on the throne, or the will of God.

GOD PERFORMS MIRACLES

*I will meditate on all your works
and consider all your mighty deeds.
Your ways, O God, are holy ... You
are the God who performs
miracles; you display your
power among the peoples.*
Psalm 77:12-14 NIV

The Shepherd laughed too ... "I don't
know anything more exhilarating and
delightful than turning weakness into
strength, and fear into faith, and that
which has been marred into perfection."

AUGUST

LOVE ONE ANOTHER

*This is what God says we must do:
Believe on the name of his Son Jesus
Christ, and love one another.*
1 John 3:23 TLB

When the Holy Spirit of love dwells in us he teaches us how to use all our faculties and all the members of our body in harmony with the law of holy love. This is the salvation which Christ offers.

AUGUST 2

A NEW NAME

*You will be called by a new name
that the mouth of the Lord will
bestow. You will be a crown of
splendor in the Lord's hand, a royal
diadem in the hand of your God.*
Isaiah 62:2-3 NIV

No one understood better than he, that
growing into likeness of a new name is a
long process.

BE HAPPY

*Is your life full of difficulties and
temptations? Then be happy, for
when the way is rough, your
patience has a chance to grow.*
James 1:2-3 TLB

Longsuffering is really the lovely
quality of forgiveness and bearing con-
tentedly and joyfully the results of the
mistakes and wrongdoing of others.

AUGUST 4

HE PROTECTS THE WAY

He holds victory in store for the upright, he is a shield to those whose walk is blameless, for he guards the course of the just and protects the way of his faithful ones.
Proverbs 2:7-8 NIV

I learned that I must accept with joy all that you allowed to happen to me on the way and everything to which the path led me!

HIS GRACE

And he said unto me, My grace is sufficient for thee: for my strength is made perfect in weakness. Most gladly therefore will I rather glory in my infirmities, that the power of Christ may rest upon me.
2 Corinthians 12:9 KJV

He wanted weakness – who was so weak as I? He promised that his grace, that wonderful, transforming grace into which I had just been lifted, would prove sufficient all the time.

AUGUST 6

LIFTED UP

But I, when I am lifted up from the earth, will draw all men to myself.
John 12:32 NIV

What human being can ever enable a shrinking soul to have the faith which steps on the seeming abyss, and finds the Rock beneath? Only God can.

OUR COMFORT OVERFLOWS

Just as the sufferings of Christ flow over into our lives, so also through Christ our comfort overflows.
2 Corinthians 1:5 NIV

God, being omnipresent, so far from being apart from the world's suffering and anguish must be conscious of ... the whole sum total of it all the time and never able to escape from it. And feeling it all with the anguish of holy love.

UNBROKEN COMMUNION

Truly our fellowship is with the Father, and with his Son Jesus Christ.
1 John 1:3 KJV

Another thing which gave her continual happiness was their unbroken communion with the King ... for he was teaching them and training them.

AUGUST 9

HIS DIVINE POWER

*His divine power has given us every-
thing we need for life and godliness
through our knowledge of him who
called us by his own glory and goodness. Through these he has given us
his very great and precious promises.*
2 Peter 1:3-4 NIV

As sons and daughters of God we are
called to be partakers of the divine nature, and when we are in Christ we have
this power to transmit his thoughts and
love to others.

AUGUST 10

YOUR WILL

*Search me, O God, and know
my heart; test my thoughts. Point
out anything you find in me that
makes you sad, and lead me along
the path of everlasting life.*
Psalm 139:23-24 TLB

Only have your will and way in me,
Shepherd. Nothing else matters.

JOY, PEACE AND LOVE

*He has sent me to bind up the
brokenhearted ... to bestow on them
a crown of beauty instead of ashes,
the oil of gladness instead of
mourning, and a garment of praise
instead of a spirit of despair.*
Isaiah 61:1-3 NIV

What is real joy, the joy which cannot
be taken from us, but sorrow accepted
and transformed. What is real peace, but
struggle and strife, fear and anxiety overcome. What indeed is real love but self
love overcome and transformed into a
passion for self-giving.

AUGUST 12

A FOUNTAIN OF LIFE

*Understanding is a fountain
of life to those who have it.*
Proverbs 16:22 NIV

All she can do is gasp with wonder, awe,
and thanksgiving, and to long with all
her heart to go higher and to see and understand more.

AUGUST 13

GREAT IS OUR LORD

How good it is to sing praises to our God ... He heals the brokenhearted and binds up their wounds ... Great is our Lord and mighty in power; his understanding has no limit.
Psalm 147:1, 3, 5 NIV

We should never concentrate in thought or prayer on the faults and failings and sins and stumblings of others, but on the power of love of the Savior to heal and change.

I PROMISE TO COME

*The Lord is righteous in all his ways
and loving toward all he has made.
The Lord is near to all who call on
him, to all who call on him in truth.*
Psalm 145:17-18 NIV

I shall be able to hear you whenever you
speak to me. Whenever you call for help
I promise to come to you at once.

ALL HAVE SINNED

All have sinned and fall short of the glory of God and are justified freely by his grace through the redemption that came by Christ Jesus. God presented him as a sacrifice of atonement.
Romans 3:23-25 NIV

Whene'er you wound a son of man
The Son of God still bleeds.
And not till sin is wholly slain
Can God's own heart be healed of
pain.

AUGUST 16

GOD'S SECRET PLAN

God's secret plan ... is Christ himself. In him lie hidden all the mighty, untapped treasures of wisdom and knowledge.
Colossians 2:2-3 TLB

Truth cannot be understood from books alone or by any written words, but only by personal growth and development in understanding.

AUGUST 17

CONCEPTIONS
OF TRUTH

*The word of God is living and active,
sharper than any two-edged sword
... It is able to judge the thoughts
and intentions of the heart.*
Hebrews 4:12 NRSV

How strangely and beautifully God
illumines our understanding and gradually develops our capacity to see and understand more, so that the Scriptures
seem constantly to unfold to us new and
richer conceptions of truth as we are able
to bear it.

FILLED WITH THE SPIRIT

*Be filled with the Spirit ... Sing
and make music in your heart to
the Lord, always giving thanks to
God the Father for everything.*
Ephesians 5:18-20 NIV

A child of God must never be content
with anything short of the eternal life
of God himself, in Jesus Christ, filling
and transforming and controlling his
whole being.

A LIVING SACRIFICE

I plead with you to give your bodies to God. Let them be a living sacrifice, holy – the kind he can accept.
Romans 12:1 TLB

Sacrifice is indeed the ecstasy of giving the best we have to the One we love the most. When that is the experience of the heart, sorrow and disappointment and heartache become sweeter than the greatest natural happiness.

AUGUST 20

A NEW PERSPECTIVE

*The reverence and fear of God
are basic to all wisdom. Knowing
God results in every other kind
of understanding.*
Proverbs 9:10 TLB

She never tired of looking from the
glorious new viewpoint on the first
slopes of the Kingdom of Love and seeing it all from a new perspective.

HE LAID DOWN HIS LIFE

*I am come that ye might have life, and
that ye might have it more abundantly.
I lay down my life for the sheep.*
John 10:15 KJV

It was there, on the cross, that he laid
down his will and his life for us, and it
is there that we, too, are enabled to lay
down our will and yield our life to him,
and, in that yielding, the contact is made
which unites us to him forever.

GOD OF ALL COMFORT

*Praise be to the God and Father
of our Lord Jesus Christ, the Father
of compassion and the God of
all comfort, who comforts us in
all our troubles.*
2 Corinthians 1:3-4 NIV

The label on the bottle read, "Spirit of
Grace and Comfort," and when Much-
Afraid had taken a drop or two she felt
so revived and strengthened that she was
ready to begin the ascent.

ABIDE IN GOD

*Those who abide in love abide in
God, and God abides in them.
Love has been perfected among us.*
1 John 4:16-17 NRSV

We agree with the Lord that his Holy
Spirit is to be allowed to dwell in us and
use every faculty and power that we pos-
sess in the way that he chooses.

PERFECT PEACE

He will keep in perfect peace all those who trust in him, whose thoughts turn often to the Lord!
Isaiah 26:3 TLB

Love can never rest until real peace, which is perfect harmony with the law of love, is brought to the hearts of all men everywhere.

AUGUST 25

HAPPY TO LOVE

Love is patient, love is kind ... It is not self-seeking ... It always protects, always trusts, always hopes, always perseveres.
1 Corinthians 13:4-5, 7 NIV

But it is so happy to love," said the Shepherd quietly. "It is happy to love even if you are not loved in return."

AUGUST 26

LOVE IS OF GOD

*Beloved, let us love one another:
for love is of God: and everyone
that loveth is born of God and
knoweth God ... If we love one
another, God dwelleth in us and
his love is perfected in us.*
1 John 4:7, 12 KJV

Love is the welding flame by which the
true Church of Christ is welded together. It is love which opens our blind
eyes and enables us to see truth and to
follow on to know the Lord.

TRUST THEE AND OBEY

We must work the works of him who sent me while it is day; night is coming when no one can work.
John 9:4 NRSV

Some task thou may'st set me,
Quick or hard to fret me,
Let my heart unswerving,
Trust thee and obey.

AUGUST 28

THE ROYAL LAW

If ye fulfil the royal law according to the Scripture, Thou shalt love thy neighbour as thyself, ye shall do well.
James 2:8 KJV

There were two things which our Lord emphasized ... first, the supreme importance of faith as the only way to make contact with God; secondly, love as the one vital principle by which we maintain contact with our fellow men.

SONS OF GOD

*Behold, what manner of love the
Father hath bestowed upon us, that
we should be called the sons of God.*
1 John 3:1 KJV

We are here in order that, as sons of
God through our Lord Jesus Christ, and
by his life given to us, we may become
creative love thinkers, willers and doers
of good.

AUGUST 30

MY WITNESSES

*But you will receive power when
the Holy Spirit has come upon you;
and you will be my witnesses in
Jerusalem, in all Judea and Samaria,
and to the ends of the earth.*
Acts 1:8 NRSV

We will go down with you and speak
to them and show what you have done
for us and what you are willing and able
to do for them.

BLESSED ARE
THE MERCIFUL

*Blessed are the merciful: for
they shall obtain mercy.*
Matthew 5:7 KJV

Blessed are the merciful," the tender
and compassionate in judgment, who
will not criticize, but discern with the
eye of love where help, and perhaps warn-
ing, is needed.

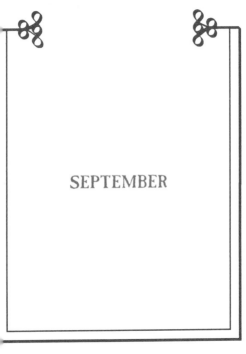

SEPTEMBER

SEPTEMBER 1

THE REALITY OF HIS PRESENCE

This is his command: to believe in the name of his Son, Jesus Christ, and to love one another as he commanded us. Those who obey his commands live in him, and he in them. And this is how we know that he lives in us: We know it by the Spirit he gave us.
1 John 3:23-24 NIV

The same overwhelming sense of the reality of his presence always followed every act of obedience.

SEEK THE LORD

*Glory in his holy name; let the hearts
of those who seek the Lord rejoice.
Seek the Lord and his strength; seek
his presence continually.*
Psalm 105:3-4 NRSV

I have not ceased to love, and Love
helped me push through the crack in the
rock until I could look right out onto
my Love the sun himself.

SEPTEMBER 3

EVERYTHING
IN THE WORLD

*For everything in the world – the
cravings of sinful man, the lust of
his eyes and the boasting of what
he has and does – comes from the
world. The world and its desires
pass away, but the man who does
the will of God lives forever.*
1 John 2:16-17 NIV

Love can never rest until all evil is overcome and swallowed up in victory.

SEPTEMBER 4

THE ONE CONNECTING LINK

Without faith it is impossible to please him: for he that cometh to God must believe that he is, and that he is a rewarder of them that diligently seek him.
Hebrews 11:6 KJV

Faith is the one connecting link by which we make contact with God. Unbelief cuts us off from God, and faith unites us with him, making us receptive of his eternal life.

SEPTEMBER 5

GRACE AND GLORY

*Jehovah God is our Light and our
Protector. He gives us grace and glory.
No good thing will he withhold from
those who walk along his paths.*
Psalm 84:11 TLB

"This is your new name," he declared.
"From henceforth you are Grace and
Glory."

SEPTEMBER 6

THE SECRET OF VICTORY

*Do not grieve the Holy Spirit of
God, with whom you were sealed for
the day of redemption ... Be imitators
of God ... and live a life of love.*
Ephesians 4:30; 5:1-2 NIV

Willingness to go the whole way and
to agree that there shall be no exceptions
to grieve the Holy Spirit of love, this
is the secret of victory.

VULNERABLE TO PAIN

Love your enemies, do good to
those who hate you, bless those
who curse you, pray for those who
mistreat you ... Do to others as
you would have them do to you.
Luke 6:27, 31 NIV

To love does mean to put yourself into
the power of the loved one and to become very vulnerable to pain.

ONE GOD

*There is but one God, the Father,
... and there is but one Lord, Jesus
Christ, through whom all things
came and through whom we live.*
1 Corinthians 8:6 NIV

I have seen the face of Jesus.
Tell me nought of earth beside.
I have heard the voice of Jesus,
And my soul is satisfied.

TRIALS INTO GLORY

It is God who arms me with strength and makes my way perfect. He makes my feet like the feet of a deer; he enables me to stand on the heights.
Psalm 18:32-33 NIV

She marveled at the grace and love and tenderness and patience which had led and trained and guarded and kept poor faltering Much-Afraid, which had not allowed her to turn back, and which now changed all her trials into glory.

IN PERFECT UNITY

*Over all these virtues put on love,
which binds them all together in perfect unity. Let the peace of Christ rule
in your hearts, since as members of
one body you were called to peace.*
Colossians 3:14-15 NIV

The basis of our unity is a Person, the
Lord Jesus Christ ... It is not our understanding of his teaching and belief in his
atoning death which unites us ... but our
longing to worship and obey him according to the light which we have.

TO THE GLORY OF GOD

We constantly pray ... that by his power he may fulfill every good purpose of yours and every act prompted by your faith. We pray this so that the name of our Lord Jesus may be glorified in you.
2 Thessalonians 1:11-12 NIV

Every trial, every test, every difficulty and seemingly wrong experience through which you may have to pass, is only another opportunity granted to you of conquering an evil thing and bringing out of it something to the lasting praise and glory of God.

SEPTEMBER 12

AN UNDIVIDED HEART

*I will give them an undivided heart
and put a new spirit in them; I will
remove from them their heart of stone
and give them a heart of flesh.*
Ezekiel 11:19 NIV

That was the natural human love which
I tore out from your heart when the time
was ripe ... so that the real Love could
grow there alone and fill your whole
heart.

SEPTEMBER 13

FULL VICTORY

*If we confess our sins, he who
is faithful and just will forgive
us our sins and cleanse us from
all unrighteousness.*
1 John 1:9 NRSV

If we are willing to make a clean sweep
without any reservations or exceptions,
then the Savior will gladly give full victory.

SEPTEMBER 14

THE KINGDOM OF GOD

The Kingdom of God isn't ushered in with visible signs ... For the Kingdom of God is within you.
Luke 17:20-21 TLB

Even now the kingdom of God is to be realized within us, in our renewed minds, as more and more fully we come under the reign and rule of the King of Love, Christ Jesus our Lord.

WHOM BUT THEE

Whom have I in heaven but thee, and there is none upon earth that I desire but thee.
Psalm 73:35 KJV

There is nothing whatever between my Love and my heart, nothing around to distract me from him. He shines upon me and makes me to rejoice.

SEPTEMBER 16

GOD IS LOVE

We will in all things grow up into him who is the Head, that is, Christ. From him the whole body, joined and held together by every supporting ligament, grows and builds itself up in love, as each part does its work.
Ephesians 4:15-16 NIV

We must be loved and we must love, for love creates and awakens love ... God is love, and God is the Creator of all, and love is the only really creative power in the universe.

LOVE WHAT IS GOOD

You love what is good and hate what is wrong. Therefore God, your God, has given you more gladness than anyone else.
Psalm 45:7 TLB

Blessed are they that hunger and thirst for righteousness with a passionate and continuous longing for rightness in thought, word and deed, and a corresponding hatred of wrongness.

RIPE FOR HARVEST

*Open your eyes and look at the
fields! They are ripe for harvest.*
John 4:35 NIV

Their very misery and loneliness and
sorrow will make them more willing to
listen to news of your grace and of your
desire to help them.

CROWNED WITH GLORY

*They will come and shout for joy
on the heights of Zion; they will
rejoice in the bounty of the Lord ...
I will turn their mourning into
gladness; I will give them comfort
and joy instead of sorrows.*
Jeremiah 31:12-13 NIV

So with a new name, and united to the
King and crowned with glory, Grace and
Glory, accompanied by her companions
and friends, came to the High Places and
was led into the Kingdom of Love.

SEPTEMBER 20

DELIVERED FROM WRONG HABITS

May my spoken words and unspoken thoughts be pleasing even to you, O Lord my Rock and my Redeemer.
Psalm 19:14 TLB

If, therefore, we sincerely long to be delivered from wrong habits of thought, we must agree at the same time to be delivered from wrong habits of speech, for the two things go together.

SEPTEMBER 21

THE FLOWER OF LOVE

*I pray that out of his glorious riches
he may strengthen you with power
through his Spirit in your inner
being, so that Christ may dwell
in you hearts through faith.*
Ephesians 3:16-17 NIV

No one is allowed to dwell in the Kingdom of Love, unless they have the flower of Love already blooming in their hearts.

A HEART LIKE THINE

*He died for all, that those who
live should no longer live for
themselves but for him who died
for them and was raised again.*
2 Corinthians 5:15 NIV

Lord Crucified, give me a heart
like thine,
Teach me to love the dying souls
of men,
And keep my heart in closest touch
with thee
And give me love, pure Calvary love
To win the lost for thee.

LOVING ONE ANOTHER

A new commandment I give unto you, That ye love one another; as I have loved you, that ye also love one another. By this shall all men know that ye are my disciples, if ye have love one to another.
John 13:34-35 KJV

If every Christian was like a burning bush on fire with love, loving one another as themselves, in spite of diversity of temperament, gifts, character, creed and doctrine, would not people be convicted at once?

SEPTEMBER 24

SONGS OF JOY

*Those who sow in tears will reap
with songs of joy. He who goes
out weeping, carrying seed to sow,
will return with songs of joy,
carrying sheaves with him.*
Psalm 126:5-6 NIV

Oh, that I may always react to sorrow
in such a way that it will be overcome
and be changed into his joy.

BEARING THE COST

*We then that are strong ought
to bear the infirmities of the weak,
and not to please ourselves.*
Romans 15:1 KJV

She said, "Oh my Lord, behold me – I
am thy little handmaiden Bearing-the-
Cost."

SEPTEMBER 26

YOUR REWARD

*Be careful not to do your 'acts of
righteousness' before men, to be
seen by them. If you do, you will have
no reward from your Father in heaven.
... Your Father, who sees what is done
in secret, will reward you.*
Matthew 6:1, 4 NIV

It is possible to share with others and
to witness to the grace and love and gentleness and power of the Savior without
at the same time drawing attention to our
own supposed rather special obedience
and sacrifice and fruitfulness!

THE LORD'S LOVE

From everlasting to everlasting the Lord's love is with those who fear him ... with those who keep his covenant and remember to obey his precepts.
Psalm 103:17-18 NIV

When we have been yielding our minds to Christ and talking to him, we also cannot fail to reveal it in some way afterwards. Thank God for this true and comforting thought.

REAL FAITH

Faith by itself, if it is not accompanied by action, is dead ... As the body without the spirit is dead, so faith without deeds is dead.
James 2:17, 26 NIV

Real faith, as the Bible conceives of it, is responsiveness to God, who has made himself known to us in Jesus Christ. And unbelief is unresponsiveness, the hardening of our wills in a refusal to respond as we ought to that which we know is true.

ENCOMPASSED BY PEACE

*In repentance and rest is
your salvation, in quietness
and trust is your strength.*
Isaiah 30:15 NIV

She felt completely encompassed by
peace, and a great inner quietness and
contentment drowned every feeling of
curiosity, loneliness and anticipation.

SEPTEMBER 30

INTERCESSION

Pray much for others; plead for God's mercy upon them; give thanks for all he is going to do for them.
1 Timothy 2:1 TLB

Intercession itself of course is thinking under the Lord's control, allowing ourselves to be shown the ideal which he wants, in ourselves and in others, and joining with him in praying and claiming that it shall come to pass.

OCTOBER

PERSECUTED FOR RIGHTEOUSNESS

*Blessed are they which are perse-
cuted for righteousness' sake: for
theirs is the kingdom of heaven.*
Matthew 5:10 KJV

"Blessed are they that are persecuted
for righteousness' sake." Those who
willingly suffer for the Lord without
self-pity or parade or bitterness.

OCTOBER 2

GOD'S MIRACLES

*The people were amazed when
they saw the mute speaking, the
crippled made well, the lame
walking and the blind seeing.
And they praised the God of Israel.*
Matthew 15:31 NIV

It was true, the ugly, twisted mouth had
vanished and the face she saw reflected
back by the water was as relaxed and perfect as the face of a little child.

OCTOBER 3

YOUR HOLY HILL

*O send out your light and your
truth; let them lead me; let them bring
me to your holy hill and to your dwelling. Then I will go to the altar of
God, to God my exceeding joy.*
Psalm 43:3-4 NRSV

As you get near the real High Places,
the air is fresh and invigorating. It
strengthens the whole body and there
are streams with wonderful healing
properties, so that those who bathe in
them find all their blemishes and dis-
figurements washed away.

OCTOBER 4

A SONG OF PRAISE

He drew me up from the desolate pit, out of the miry bog, and set my feet upon a rock, making my steps secure. He put a new song in my mouth, a song of praise to our God.
Psalm 40:2-3 NRSV

Every new test and trial which we meet is really the beginning (as the psalmist expresses it) of "learning a new song of praise unto our God."

THE PATH OF MY WILL

The Lord will keep you from all evil; he will keep your life. The Lord will keep your going out and your coming in from this time on and forevermore.
Psalm 121:7-8 NRSV

Remember that nothing can do you any real harm while you are following the path of my will.

OCTOBER 6

ALL THINGS
ARE POSSIBLE

*I can do everything God asks me
to with the help of Christ who gives
me the strength and power.*
Philippians 4:13 TLB

All things are possible to him
That can on Jesus' name believe ...
I can, I do believe in thee,
All things are possible to me.

OCTOBER 7

THOSE WHO SHARE

How does God's love abide in anyone who has the world's good and sees a brother or sister in need and yet refuses to help?
1 John 3:17 NRSV

There is one law by which we live,
"Love loves to give and give
and give!" ...
No lasting joy is anywhere
Save in the hearts of those who share.

OCTOBER 8

ONENESS

We have put our hope in the living God, who is the Savior of all men, and especially of those who believe.
1 Timothy 4:10 NIV

To love is to recognize our oneness with all whom God has created, and to have a passionate desire to realize this oneness fully.

OCTOBER 9

FINISH THE RACE

*I consider my life worth nothing
to me, if only I may finish the race
and complete the task the Lord Jesus
has given me – the task of testifying
to the gospel of God's grace.*
Acts 20:24 NIV

She had only one desire in her heart,
to reach the place appointed and fulfill
the command which had been given her.

SHINE LIKE STARS

Do all things without murmuring and arguing, so that you may be blameless and innocent, children of God without blemish in the midst of a crooked and perverse generation, in which you shine like stars in the world.
Philippians 2:14-15 NRSV

Why should a child of God who has the unutterable privilege of living in heaven, be heard grumbling about the weather on earth?

WHAT LIES BEYOND

We can see and understand only a little about God now ... Someday we are going to see him in his completeness, face to face.
1 Corinthians 13:12 TLB

The glorious view which they now enjoyed was but small in comparison with all that lay beyond, and would be visible only from yet higher places above.

THE EYES OF OUR UNDERSTANDING

Give me understanding, that I may keep your law and observe it with my whole heart. Lead me in the path of your commandments, for I delight in it.
Psalm 119:34-35 NRSV

Let us encourage one another to go exploring further along the way of glad obedience to God and acceptance of his will, whereby the eyes of our understanding will be enlightened.

A GROWING JOY

For you shall go out in joy, and be led back in peace; the mountains and the hills before you shall burst into song, and all the trees of the field shall clap their hands.
Isaiah 55:12 NRSV

She stood looking about her, her heart leaping and thrilling with a growing joy which was beyond her understanding and a peace indescribably sweet which seemed to enfold her.

NO FEARS

There is no fear in love; but perfect love casteth out fear ... He that feareth is not made perfect in love.
1 John 4:18 KJV

Those mountains on the other side of the river are the borderland of my Father's Kingdom, the Realm of Love. No Fears of any kind are able to live there because "perfect love casteth out fear."

OCTOBER 15

LOVE NEVER ENDS

Love is patient; love is kind; love is not envious or boastful or arrogant or rude. It does not insist on its own way; it is not irritable or resentful; it does not rejoice in wrongdoing, but rejoices in the truth. It bears all things, believes all things, hopes all things, endures all things. Love never ends.
1 Corinthians 13:4-8 NRSV

Love accepts with joy all that God's will permits to happen to us. Love bears and forgives all that others do to us. Love creates goodness through creative love thinking.

OCTOBER 16

THE CHOSEN ONES

*You are the children of the Lord
your God ... You are a people
holy to the Lord your God. Out of
all the peoples on the face of the
earth, the Lord has chosen you to
be his treasured possession.*
Deuteronomy 14:1-2 NIV

Unless you sons and daughters of men
are loved and also love all others beside
yourselves, you cannot become what you
are destined to be, the sons and daughters of the God who is love.

RIVERS OF LIVING WATER

Let anyone who is thirsty come to me, and let the one who believes in me drink. As the scripture has said, "Out of the believers's heart shall flow rivers of living water."
John 7:37-38 NRSV

I was forced to thrust deeper and deeper into the river of his love and grace, for the sources of my spiritual life no longer lay near the surface.

OUR REFUGE AND STRENGTH

God is our refuge and strength, a very present help in trouble. Therefore we will not fear, though the earth should change ... though its waters roar and foam, though the mountains tremble with its tumult.
Psalm 46:1-3 NRSV

Throughout the whole storm she was filled with a strange and wonderful peace such as she had never felt before.

WHY WORRY

Why worry about a speck in the eye of a brother when you have a board in your own? ... Hypocrite! First get rid of the board. Then you can see to help your brother.
Matthew 7:3, 5 TLB

It is never well to speak of personal faults or irritating matters, unless there has first been a time of coming to the Lord together in united silence, humility, and faith.

OCTOBER 20

THE LORD'S DISCIPLINE

*Do not despise the Lord's discipline
or be weary of his reproof, for the Lord
reproves the one he loves, as a father
the son in whom he delights.*
Proverbs 3:11-12 NRSV

That is why a parent must punish a
child, that he may learn not to wrong or
harm others, and to discipline his nature
and learn self-control.

OCTOBER 21

THE WILL OF THE LORD

Do not be foolish, but understand what the will of the Lord is ... Be filled with the Spirit.
Ephesians 5:17-18 NRSV

Faith is the response of our wills to the will of God. It is willingness to see God's will and willingness to obey it.

YOUR HEART'S DESIRE

The ransomed of the Lord will return.
They will enter Zion with singing;
everlasting joy will crown their heads.
Gladness and joy will overtake them,
and sorrow and sighing will flee away.
Isaiah 51:11 NIV

Dare to begin to be happy. If you will go forward in the way before you, you will soon receive the promise, and I will give you your heart's desire.

OCTOBER 23

GOD'S TEMPLE

*Don't you know that you yourselves
are God's temple and that God's Spirit
lives in you? ... God's temple is sacred,
and you are that temple.*
1 Corinthians 3:16-17 NIV

Yes, every soul a temple is
Wherein love plans to dwell,
And each must make its choice
for this –
To be a heaven or hell.

THERE IS ONE JUDGE

*There is one lawgiver and judge
who is able to save you and to
destroy. So who, then, are
you to judge your neighbor?*
James 4:12 NRSV

We are all so different, we must remember that what is real and helpful to
one person is not so to another. So we
must not judge one another.

OCTOBER 25

A GOD OF JUSTICE

The Lord longs to be gracious to
you; he rises to show you compassion.
For the Lord is a God of justice.
Blessed are all who wait for him.
Isaiah 30:18 NIV

His eyes were still full of gentleness
and tenderness but also of strength and
power and authority.

OCTOBER 26

I WILL NOT BE AFRAID

He has said, "I will never leave you or forsake you." So we can say with confidence, "The Lord is my helper; I will not be afraid."
Hebrews 13:5-6 NRSV

"Don't be afraid," said the Shepherd gently. "You are in my service."

ETERNAL THINGS

*We look not at what can be seen
but at what cannot be seen; for
what can be seen is temporary, but
what cannot be seen is eternal.*
2 Corinthians 4;18 NRSV

The noblest and most glorious and
most blessed function of the imagination is to make it possible for the
invisible and eternal things to become
real to us.

OCTOBER 28

"I ABIDE IN HIM"

Whoever obeys his word, truly in this person the love of God has reached perfection. By this we may be sure that we are in him: whoever says, "I abide in him," ought to walk just as he walked.
1 John 2:5-6 NRSV

"I am love," said the King very clearly. "If you want to see the pattern of true love, look at me, for I am the expression of the law of love."

OCTOBER 29

THE LOVE ENERGY

*Fan into flame the gift of God, which
is in you through the laying on of
my hands. For God did not give us
a spirit of timidity, but a spirit of
power, of love and of self discipline.*
2 Timothy 1:6-7 NIV

We are so created by the God of Love,
from whom we derive our very being,
that nothing can perfectly satisfy us until we are enabled to turn all the love
energy outward in universal love to God
and to all men.

LIGHT HAS DAWNED

*The people who sat in darkness
have seen a great light, and for those
who sat in the region and shadow
of death light has dawned.*
Matthew 4:16 NRSV

With his coming the mist was rapidly
clearing away and a real gleam of sun-
shine – the first they had seen for days
– broke through at last.

OCTOBER 31

THANKS BE TO GOD

*The sting of death is sin, and the
power of sin is the law. But thanks be
to God! He gives us the victory
through our Lord Jesus Christ.*
1 Corinthians 15:56-57 NIV

He is able to overcome triumphantly
all the awful power of sin's disease in
the human race and to overrule all its
ghastly effect and results, and to recon-
cile all things to God.

NOVEMBER

LOVE ONE ANOTHER

Beloved, if God so loved us, we ought also to love one another. No man hath seen God at any time. If we love one another, God dwelleth in us, and his love is perfected in us.
1 John 4:11-12 KJV

Our Lord summed up the whole nature of love in the one commandment that he gave us. "That ye love one another as I have loved you."

NOVEMBER 2

LEAD HOME

*Let me live that I may praise
you ... I have gone astray like a
lost sheep; seek out your servant,
for I do not forget your commands.*
Psalm 119:175-176 NRSV

O thou from whom my spirit came,
And wanders in this wild,
Behold I bear thy lovely name,
Lead home thy wandering child.

YOUR STATUTES

*Your statutes are my heritage
forever; they are the joy of my
heart. My heart is set on keeping
your decrees to the very end.*
Psalm 119:111-112 NIV

So I learned ... the one vital principle
of the hearing heart, namely, that one
must keep in closest contact with him
and be willing to obey at any cost.

KNEEL BEFORE THE LORD

O come, let us worship and bow down, let us kneel before the Lord, our Maker! For he is our God, and we are the people of his pasture, and the sheep of his hand.
Psalm 95:6-7 NRSV

As Much-Afraid bowed herself and knelt at his feet to worship, the face that looked down upon her was that of the Shepherd whom she had loved and followed from the very low places up to the heights.

A LAMB WITHOUT BLEMISH

It was not with perishable things such as silver or gold that you were redeemed ... but with the precious blood of Christ, a lamb without blemish or defect. He was chosen before the creation of the world, but was revealed in these last times for your sake.
1 Peter 1:18-21 NIV

In the four Gospels we have a most beautifully true and lifelike portrait of our Lord and Savior ... of himself, his character, his reactions to every conceivable circumstance and person.

NOVEMBER 6

THE BLOOD OF JESUS

*If we walk in the light as he himself
is in the light, we have fellowship with
one another, and the blood of Jesus
his Son cleanses us from all sin.*
1 John 1:7 NRSV

I never think of you as you are now but
as you will be when I have brought you
to the Kingdom of Love and washed you
from all the stains and defilements of
the journey.

ACCEPTANCE OF HIS WILL

*Continue to work out your salvation
with fear and trembling, for it is God
who works in you to will and to act
according to his good purpose.*
Philippians 2:12-13 NIV

Every acceptance of his will becomes
an altar of sacrifice, and every such sur-
render and abondonment of ourselves to
his will is a means of furthering us on
the way to the High Places.

NOVEMBER 8

ONENESS

*I have given them the glory that
you gave me, that they may be one
as we are one: I in them and you in
me. May they be brought to complete
unity to let the world know that you
sent me and have loved them even
as you have loved me.*
John 17:22-23 NIV

There is one unique characteristic and
quality in true love, which is the hall-
mark and guarantee of the real thing.
Love is a passionate desire for oneness.

HOLINESS

*I am the Lord your God;
consecrate yourselves and be
holy, because I am holy.*
Leviticus 11:44 NIV

Holiness and happiness and health are the result of complete separation from everything which breaks the law of love, and a holy people are those who are set apart to love.

NOTHING CAN SEPARATE US

Nothing will ever be able to separate us from the love of God demonstrated by our Lord Jesus Christ when he died for us.
Romans 8:39 TLB

We know that we face nothing alone, neither temptation, test or trial, and that nothing can separate us from the presence and love of Christ or from contact with his power.

NOVEMBER 11

THE PEACEMAKERS

*Blessed are the peacemakers: for they
shall be called the children of God.*
Matthew 5:9 KJV

"Blessed are the peacemakers." Those
who delight in ending strife and discord
and have a horror of sowing seeds of sus-
picion and dislike.

HE WAS TRANSFIGURED

*And he was transfigured before them,
and his face shone like the sun, and
his clothes became dazzling white.*
Matthew 17:2 NRSV

The King of Love himself ... was
clothed in a white garment glistening in
its purity. but over it he wore a robe of
purple and blue and scarlet studded with
gold and precious gems.

NOVEMBER 13

BELIEVE

"Sirs, what must I do to be saved?"
They replied, "Believe in the Lord
Jesus, and you will be saved."
Acts 16:30-31 NIV

It is the Shepherd himself. Open the door and tell him to come in!

LORD OF HEAVEN AND EARTH

The God who made the world and everything in it is the Lord of heaven and earth and does not live in temples built by hands ... as if he needed anything, because he himself gives all men life and breath and everything else.
Acts 17:24-25 NIV

I said haltingly in Hebrew and groping for the right words, "No, the God I worship is not a stone, nor a cross of wood."

THE PLACE WHERE YOU DWELL

Send forth your light and your truth, let them guide me; let them bring me to your holy mountain, to the place where you dwell. Then will I go to the altar of God, to God, my joy and my delight.
Psalm 43:3-4 NIV

Never doubt that the High Places are there, towering up above you, and be quite sure that whatever happens I mean to bring you up there exactly as I have promised.

NOVEMBER 16

IN THE DAYS OF YOUR YOUTH

Remember your Creator in the days of your youth ... Fear God and keep his commandments, for this is the whole duty of man.
Ecclesiastes 12:1, 13 NIV

If all young Christians are taught to keep the daily quiet time with their Lord, to speak to him personally and to learn to hear his voice speaking to them, then their spiritual senses will become developed.

FORGIVE

*Do not judge, and you will not
be judged. Do not condemn, and
you will not be condemned.
Forgive, and you will be forgiven.*
Luke 6:37 NIV

If there is one sin in the thought life
more common than another, it is this
brooding ... on the shortcomings, blemishes, failures and mistakes of others,
until they ... crush the thoughts of love
in a truly awful way.

LOVE HIM

What does the Lord your God require of you? Only to fear the Lord your God, to walk in all his ways, to love him, to serve the Lord your God with all your heart and with all your soul, and to keep the commandments of the Lord your God.
Deuteronomy 10:12-13 NRSV

I must love you as long as I continue to exist. I cannot live without loving you.
– Much-Afraid.

ACCEPT HIS TEACHING

Teach me, O Lord, to follow your decrees; then I will keep them to the end. Give me understanding, and I will keep your law and obey it with all my heart. Direct me in the path of your commands, for there I find delight.
Psalm 119:30-32 NIV

The loveliest and most glorious place in all the universe is the point where we contact him, our Lord and Savior, and accept his teaching as the standard by which we are to live.

A GLORIOUS OPPORTUNITY

Suffering produces endurance, and endurance produces character, and character produces hope, and hope does not disappoint us, because God's love has been poured into our hearts through the Holy Spirit.
Romans 5:3-5 NRSV

We know ... that even the most unjust and cruel things, as well as all seemingly pointless and undeserved sufferings, have been permitted by God as a glorious opportunity ... to produce in us, little by little, his own lovely character.

NOVEMBER 21

FAITH

Now faith is the substance of things hoped for, the evidence of things not seen.
Hebrews 11:1 KJV

Who that has not experienced it can even begin to understand the joy, the security, the blessed sense of the immense worthwhileness of life, developed by living in the invisible world where all things are eternal.

NOVEMBER 22

THY HOLY HILL

Who shall ascend the hill of the Lord? And who shall stand in his holy place? Those who have clean hands and pure hearts, who did not lift up their souls to what is false.
Psalm 24:3-4 NRSV

Send forth thy truth,
O shining Light,
That I may follow till
I come at last, before the night,
Up to thy holy hill.

NOVEMBER 23

FIX YOUR EYES ON JESUS

Let us fix our eyes on Jesus, the author and perfecter of our faith, who for the joy set before him endured the cross, scorning its shame, and sat down at the right hand of the throne of God.
Hebrews 12:2 NIV

When we look at the Lord Jesus as he is revealed to us in the Gospels, we have a true and perfect portrait of Love himself and a trustworthy standard and pattern by which to judge everything which calls itself love.

HE HAS APPOINTED ME

*The Spirit of the Lord is upon me;
he has appointed me to preach
Good News to the poor.*
Luke 4:18 TLB

Whenever I preach or speak about him
I know that love, the joy and ecstasy of
it, and an immense compassion.

SING PRAISES

*It is a good thing to give thanks
unto the Lord, and to sing praises
unto thy name, O most High.*
Psalm 92:1 KJV

A Christian is one who reacts to everything with praise and thanksgiving and joy, and thereby receives power to bring good out of evil.

NOVEMBER 26

FROM DEATH UNTO LIFE

He that heareth my word, and believeth on him that sent me, hath everlasting life, and shall not come into condemnation; but is passed from death unto life.
John 5:24 KJV

Let us love and fruitful be.
Love is God's own breath.
Love will kindle love and see
New life born from death.

NOVEMBER 27

THE GREAT OPENER

*This is my prayer: that your love
may abound more and more in
knowledge and depth of insight,
so that you may be able to discern
what is best and may be pure and
blameless until the day of Christ.*
Philippians 1:9-10 NIV

It is love, and not intellectual learning,
which leads us on into all truth. Love is
the great opener of the understanding.

NOVEMBER 28

GUIDE ME

*Show me your ways, O Lord, teach me
your paths; guide me in your truth and
teach me, for you are God my Savior,
and my hope is in you all day long.*
Psalm 25:4-5 NIV

Always go forward along the path of
obedience as far as you know it until I
intervene, even if it seems to be leading
you where you fear I could never mean
for you to go.

THE ONE BASIC LAW

*Love the Lord your God with all
your heart, soul, and mind.*
Matthew 22:37 TLB

Love is the one basic law on which the whole universe is founded, and by obeying that law, everything abides in harmony, perfect joy and perfect fruitfulness.

NOVEMBER 30

FOR OUR GOOD

We know that all that happens to us is working for our good if we love God.
Romans 8:28 TLB

All that happens to us (even the results of our own folly, stupidity and sin, as well as the results of the follies, stupidities and sins of others), all consitute a God-permitted opportunity to bring good out of evil.

DECEMBER

DECEMBER 1

KNOWING CHRIST JESUS

I regard everything as loss because of the surpassing value of knowing Christ Jesus my Lord. For his sake I have suffered the loss of all things ... in order that I may gain Christ and be found in him.
Philippians 3:8-9 NRSV

Will you go down this path of forgiveness into the Valley of Loss, just because it is the way that I have chosen for you? Will you still trust and still love me?

MY SOUL WAITETH

*My soul waiteth for the Lord more
than they that watch for the morning: I say, more than they that
watch for the morning.*
Psalm 130:6 KJV

As in the early morning
The snowy mountain peaks
Look up to greet the dawning,
So my heart longs and seeks
To see thy face
And glow with grace.

ABOVE ALL ELSE

Listen: Jehovah is our God, Jehovah alone. You must love him with all your heart, soul, and might.
Deuteronomy 6:4-5 TLB

This instinct for love, so firmly implanted in the human heart, is the supreme way by which we learn to desire and love God himself above all else.

DECEMBER 4

YOUR TRUTH

Test me, O Lord, and try me, exa-
mine my heart and my mind; for
your love is ever before me, and I
walk continually in your truth.
Psalm 26:2-3 NIV

He blesses and confirms and makes
fruitful all truth wherever he finds it.

PURE CALVARY LOVE

*Many waters cannot quench love;
rivers cannot wash it away. If one were
to give all the wealth of his house for
love, it would be utterly scorned.*
Song of Songs 8:7 NIV

I did not really know what holy love was, nor what it would mean if I suddenly found myself immersed in what I had so often sung about, "pure Calvary love, which wins the lost to Thee."

DECEMBER 6

I LOOK TO YOU

*Each morning I will look to you
in heaven and lay my requests
before you, praying earnestly.*
Psalms 5:3 TLB

Here like the peaks at sunrise
My mind to thee I raise;
Clothe me with glory likewise
Make me to burn with praise.

THE CHEERFUL HEART

*A happy heart makes the face
cheerful ... the cheerful heart
has a continual feast.*
Proverbs 15:13,15 NIV

She went on bustling about, filling cups and attending to the wants of everyone, and was, without in the least realizing it, next to the Chief Shepherd himself, the most cheering and heartwarming person in the room.

DECEMBER 8

UNIVERSAL LOVE

Ye have heard that it hath been said, Thou shalt love thy neighbour, and hate thine enemy. But I say unto you, Love your enemies, bless them that curse you, do good to them that hate you, and pray for them which despitefully use you, and persecute you.
Matthew 5:43-44 KJV

The sign of true love, we remember, is that it is universal love, love to all, without exception, not just to a chosen few.

DECEMBER 9

HUMBLE YOURSELVES

*If my people, which are called by
my name, shall humble themselves,
and pray, and seek my face, and turn
from their wicked ways; then will I
hear from heaven, and will forgive
their sin, and will heal their land.*
2 Chronicles 7:14 KJV

It is the loveliest movement in the
world, as though to cast oneself down
is to abandon oneself to ecstasy and joy
indescribable.

DECEMBER 10

FULNESS OF JOY

Thou wilt show me the path of life: in thy presence is fulness of joy; at thy right hand there are pleasures for evermore.
Psalm 16:11 KJV

Oh, what a life of wonderful joy, adventure, and ever-deepening love the Good Shepherd leads us all to!

DECEMBER 11

THE ROYAL LAW

If you really keep the royal law found in Scripture, "Love your neighbor as yourself," you are doing right ... Judgment without mercy will be shown to anyone who has not been merciful.
James 2:8, 13 NIV

Just go on loving: it always wins in the end.
– Mrs. Valiant

TURN FEAR INTO FAITH

A windstorm arose on the sea, so great that the boat was being swamped by the waves ... And he said to them, "Why are you afraid, you of little faith?" Then he got up and rebuked the winds and the sea; and there was a dead calm.
Matthew 8:24, 26 NRSV

Turn every fear into faith at once, and look what an advantage you have! Endless opportunities of putting God's gracious promises to the test and of trusting him.

HE LOVED US

*This is love: not that we loved God,
but that he loved us and sent his Son
as an atoning sacrifice for our sins.*
1 John 4:10 NIV

She really had but one passionate
desire, not for the things which the
Shepherd had promised, but for himself.

DECEMBER 14

REACT IN LOVE

*So we do not lose heart. Even
though our outer nature is wasting
away, our inner nature is being
renewed day by day. For this slight
momentary affliction is preparing
us for an eternal weight of glory.*
2 Corinthians 4:16-17 NRSV

It is not the things which happen to us,
but our reaction to them which is important; and it is by seeking to react
always in love that the kingdom of God
reveals its presence within us.

DECEMBER 15

OVERCOMING
THE WORLD

*Everyone born of God overcomes
the world. This is the victory that
has overcome the world, even our
faith. Who is it that overcomes the
world? Only he who believes that
Jesus is the Son of God.*
1 John 5:4-5 NIV

To learn the secret of victorious living
has been the heart's desire of those who
love the Lord, in every generation.

DECEMBER 16

A FLAMING TORCH
OF LOVE

This is how we know what love is:
Jesus Christ laid down his life for us.
And we ought to lay down our lives
for our brothers ... God is love.
1 John 3:16; 4:16 NIV

You have been needing to know me as Love – not only as Redeemer and Savior, but by my real name of Love ... You too must walk in the fire of my love and become a flaming torch of love yourself.

DECEMBER 17

ONE BODY IN CHRIST

*So we, who are many, are one
body in Christ, and indivi-
dually we are members one of
another. We have gifts that differ.*
Romans 12:5-6 NRSV

In love and devotion to him we can feel
ourselves united to one another also,
even though we find we are so made that
we need to express that love, devotion
and obedience in many differing ways
and forms.

DECEMBER 18

SET APART

Put off your old self, which is being corrupted by its deceitful desires ... Put on the new self, created to be like God in true righteousness and holiness.
Ephesians 4:22, 24 NIV

Holiness ... means to be separated and set apart; separated, in fact, from all that is not love and set apart for one purpose only, that the Spirit of Holy Love may dwell in us.

DECEMBER 19

DIVINE SELF-GIVING

*My command is this: Love
each other as I have loved you.*
John 15:12 NIV

To love as he loves, and so to be an echo
– faint and feeble, but a true one – of
that eternal self, giving us drops of the
water of life, poured out in the cataract
of that divine self-giving.

DECEMBER 20

PRACTICE AND
DEVELOP FAITH

*Are not two sparrows sold for a
penny? Yet not one of them will fall
to the ground apart from your Father.
... So do not be afraid; you are of
more value than many sparrows.*
Matthew 10:29, 31 NRSV

No one has such a perfect opportunity
to practice and develop faith as do those
who must learn constantly to turn fear
into faith.

TRANSFORMED

*The body that is sown is perishable,
it is raised imperishable; it is sown
in dishonor, it is raised in glory; it
is sown in weakness, it is raised in
power; it is sown a natural body,
it is raised a spiritual body.*
1 Corinthians 15:42-44 NIV

The very characteristics and weaknesses
of temperament ... which often seem to
us to be the greatest of all hindrances to
the Christian life, are, in reality, the very
things which ... can be transformed into
their exact opposites and can produce in
us the loveliest of all qualities.

DECEMBER 22

WITHOUT STAIN
OR BLEMISH

Christ loved the church and gave himself up for her to make her holy, cleansing her by the washing with water through the word, and to present her to himself as a radiant church, without stain or blemish, but holy and blameless.
Ephesians 5:25-27 NIV

Love is beautiful, but it is also terrible – terrible in its determination to allow nothing blemished or unworthy to remain in the beloved.

DECEMBER 23

REDEEMED AND PURIFIED

He it is who gave himself for us that he might redeem us from all iniquity and purify for himself a people of his own who are zealous for good deeds.
Titus 2:14 NRSV

God is holy love, a fire of love which consumes and destroys all that is antagonistic to the nature of holy love, and which purifies and liberates into a new kind of life all who receive the nature of the fire into themselves.

DECEMBER 24

THE TRUE LIGHT

In him was life, and that life was the light of men ... The true light that gives light to every man was coming into the world. He was in the world, and though the world was made through him, the world did not recognize him.
John 1:4, 9-10 NIV

The incarnation was for this one great purpose, that we human beings might be united to God through Jesus Christ our Lord, who is the Son of God and Son of Man, the meeting place where eternal life can break through to us.

DECEMBER 25

GOOD TIDINGS

The angel said unto them, Fear not: for, behold, I bring you good tidings of great joy, which shall be to all people. For unto you is born this day in the city of David a Saviour, which is Christ the Lord.
Luke 2:10-11 KJV

Perfect Love has been manifested to the world, and the name he bears is Jesus (Savior) because his Saviorhood is the most perfect expression of love – of himself.

THE LOWEST PLACE

Christ Jesus: Who, being in very nature God ... made himself nothing, taking the very nature of a servant, being made in human likeness ... He humbled himself and became obedient to death – even death on a cross!
Philippians 2:5-8 NIV

From the highest place in the universe, the divine Love leaped down to the lowest place of all.

DECEMBER 27

MOUNTAINS OF DIFFICULTY

After you have suffered a little while, our God, who is full of kindness through Christ, will ... come and pick you up ... and make you stronger than ever.
1 Peter 5:10 TLB

There are no obstacles which our Savior's love cannot overcome, and ... to him, mountains of difficulty are as easy as an asphalt road!

CORRECT ME, LORD

*I know it is not within the power
of man to map his life and plan
his course – so you correct me,
Lord; but please be gentle.*
Jeremiah 10:23-24 TLB

Always begin to obey, and after every
new step ask if it is his will that we
should keep going forward.

SINLESS AND PERFECT

He is able to keep you from slipping and falling away, and to bring you, sinless and perfect, into his glorious presence with mighty shouts of everlasting joy.
Jude 25 TLB

Love is a consuming fire. It is a burning, unquenchable passion for the blessedness and happiness, and, above all, for the perfection of the beloved object.

DECEMBER 30

A LIFE OF LOVE

*Be imitators of God, therefore, as
dearly loved children and live a life
of love, just as Christ loved us and
gave himself up for us as a fragrant
offering and sacrifice to God.*
Ephesians 5:1-2 NIV

It is better to go stumbling and weeping and crawling like a worm along the way of love than to give it up and choose some other way.

LIVING LIGHT

*If you follow me, you won't be
stumbling through the darkness, for
living light will flood your path.*
John 8:12 TLB

As we follow him along the path of
life, let us leave him to choose every step
of the way, as we live in his radiant presence and are ever led to still higher
places.